Studies in Modern History

VIETNAM

STUDIES IN MODERN HISTORY

The Cold War, Hugh Higgins
Vietnam, Hugh Higgins

VIETNAM

HUGH HIGGINS

HEINEMANN EDUCATIONAL BOOKS

Heinemann Educational Books Ltd
LONDON EDINBURGH MELBOURNE AUCKLAND TORONTO
HONG KONG SINGAPORE KUALA LUMPUR
IBADAN NAIROBI JOHANNESBURG NEW DELHI

ISBN 0 435 31396 7
Paperback ISBN 0 435 31398 3

Published by Heinemann Educational Books Ltd
48 Charles Street, London W1X 8AH

Filmset and Printed in Great Britain by
Cox & Wyman Ltd
London, Fakenham and Reading

PREFACE

Two years ago a group of journalists working in the British press, radio and television examined the treatment by those media of the Vietnam War. They concluded that there had been and still was an overwhelming bias in favour of the official American line. Additionally, they contended that 'while the bias of the British media is bad enough in itself, the way in which they claim to offer a balanced approach makes it even worse. It also helps to more effectively delude and mystify the general public, at home and abroad, which has been led to believe in this fiction.' While recognizing that there had been some accurate reporting they noted that 'only those who are already well informed, and have time to spare, can be expected to sort the occasional wheat from the deluge of chaff.'[*]

One of my reasons for writing this book was to offer readers a chance to review the past three decades of Vietnamese history from a standpoint other than that of successive British governments. Both Conservative and Labour administrations have consistently accepted the US State Department's interpretation of events. They have largely ignored the substantial critique of that view presented by numerous unofficial American commentators. This account has attempted to give due weight to the work of, for example, Chomsky, Fitzgerald and Halberstam and to make some of their findings more accessible to British students. I hope it may encourage them to look critically at an important subject and help them to distinguish the wheat from the chaff.

Hugh Higgins
June 1975

[*] See *The British Press and Vietnam*, Indochina Solidarity Conference (1973) p. 3.

ACKNOWLEDGEMENTS

The author and publishers would like to thank the following for permission to reproduce photographs and cartoons:

Camera Press: figs. 1, 2, 5, 6, 7, 8, 9, 11, 12, 15, 21
Etablissment Cinématographique des Armées: fig. 3
Paul Popper: fig. 4
Associated Press: fig. 10
Romano Cagnoni: fig. 13
New Statesman: fig. 14
The Observer: fig. 16
Eupra Press: fig. 17
Abbas/Rex Features: fig. 18
Keystone Press: fig. 19
Miami News: fig. 20

CONTENTS

1 The impact of French rule: opposition to the French   1

2 The war against the French 1946–54   13

3 The failure of the Geneva settlement: the rule of Ngo Dinh Diem in the South   27

4 The development of the North: resistance to Diem   41

5 Kennedy and the growing American involvement   51

6 Johnson's war   66

7 The devastation of Vietnam   82

8 The effect of the war on the United States   95

9 Nixon's continuing pursuit of victory   108

10 Peace and war   123

    Appendix: Dienbienphu   135

    References   137

    Bibliography   147

    Index   150

THE IMPACT OF FRENCH RULE: OPPOSITION TO THE FRENCH

In the twentieth century proponents of empire have commonly underestimated the power of nationalism. Their misjudgment is nowhere more evident than in the recent history of Vietnam. Political leaders both in France and the United States have, through contempt for their nationalist opponents, made crucial decisions about Vietnam without the slightest understanding of the actual situation. They viewed the country in terms of its relevance to French or American interests, seemingly unaware that Vietnam could not be understood without reference to its own history and culture. It was, admittedly, a land remote from their experience. One historian has indeed claimed that 'culturally Vietnam is quite beyond the normal range of occidental comprehension'.[1]

The hackneyed image of the inscrutable orient was the product of an imperialist mentality. The fact was that empire-builders from the West made little effort to comprehend the societies they conquered. Their task was not to understand the 'natives' but to transform them. Non-white societies were considered to be under-developed both materially and culturally; only contact with the West could overcome their backwardness. Such ethnocentric convictions of white superiority have proved exceedingly tenacious. They were exemplified by President Lyndon Johnson when, shortly after launching his attack on North Vietnam, he explained how American technology would help to release the peoples of Southeast Asia from impoverishment. 'I want,' he declared, 'to leave the footprints of America there. We're going to turn the Mekong into a Tennessee Valley.'[2]

Johnson and his advisers failed to understand that basic changes in the Vietnamese way of life could be achieved only by forward-looking people from Vietnam itself. Such people, being fully conscious of the obscurantism of traditional Vietnamese society, had no illusions about the size of the problem. They themselves rejected ancestor-worship and the Confucian notion that an emperor, the Son of Heaven, should be obeyed as the mediator between heaven and the people. At the same time they appreciated that the culture based on Confucian principles had, for a thousand years, helped to propagate and maintain a sense of national identity among the Vietnamese people. The disintegration of that culture during the latter part of the nineteenth century had set them adrift. The challenge of the twentieth century was to put Vietnam on a new course, to create a new society which would have the cohesion but not the social injustice of the old.

Before recording the struggles of the reformers it is necessary to look back briefly to the end of the old society. Its destruction was the work of the French, whose incursion into Vietnam formed part of a take-over of most of Asia by Western imperialists and whose superior technology gave them control of all Indochina within a generation. Between 1858 and 1859 they occupied the area around Saigon. From 1861 they encroached on Cochinchina (the southern part of Vietnam) which they controlled by 1885. During 1883–4 they established their protectorate over the northern and central parts of the country. In the course of conquering Cochinchina they also incorporated the neighbouring kingdom of Cambodia into their empire as a protectorate. Towards the end of the century, in 1893, they compelled the Siamese government to cede the territory of Laos. Occupation of Siam itself was prevented only by imperial rivalry between France and Britain. The British had annexed Upper Burma in 1886 and were concerned about French activities in that area, since they wished to avoid a common frontier between British India and French Indochina. Siam was, therefore, allowed to remain as an independent buffer state.

In Vietnam colonization proceeded rapidly and thoroughly, its several aspects reflecting the aims of the various factions in French colonialism. Missionary groups of the powerful Roman Catholic Church wished to spread the gospel among the heathen. Merchants and financiers sought profit from the exploitation of natural resources. Ambitious politicians and administrators aspired to 'leave the footprints' of France in a backward land. To achieve their objectives the French assumed control of Vietnam's political system and refashioned its commercial and economic structure.

The political system was radically changed, despite the façade of continuity provided by the emperor, who retained some of the trappings of the Son of Heaven. He was, in fact, powerless and the mandarins, who previously had ruled on his behalf, now worked for his colonial masters. The Confucian system itself was undermined with the encouragement of Catholic missionaries, the putative leaders of 'la mission civilisatrice'. Since time immemorial the Vietnamese had been socialized in the belief that their ancestors were the source of their lives and their civilization. Worship of their ancestors was bound up with their feelings towards the land itself which, as the resting place of their fore-bears, was held sacred. The people 'flowed over the land like water, maintaining and fructifying it for the generations to come'.[3] Thus, in attacking the 'heathen' practice of ancestor-worship, mission-aries threatened to disrupt the entire life-style of the vast majority of the Vietnamese people.

The economic changes were also far-reaching. A predomin-antly agricultural society, providing a bare subsistence for the mass of peasants, did not offer sufficient scope for foreign capitalists who, therefore, attempted an economic transformation. The 1860s saw an enormous increase in the rice paddies of Cochin-china and the growth of a large export trade in rice. (By the 1930s Cochinchina was the world's third largest rice exporter, after Burma and Siam.) Industry also expanded. At the turn of the century there was increasing investment in the mining of coal and other minerals: the production of coal, tin and zinc accelerated rapidly in the period after the First World War. Later – in the 1930s – the development of extensive plantations resulted in a substan-tial export trade in rubber.[4]

Such changes were intended to create in Indochina an economic enterprise exploitable by the mother country. A few figures help to illustrate how far they succeeded. In 1938, two years before their Indochinese empire was overwhelmed by the Japanese, the French provided 95 per cent of the European capital invested in business enterprises and all the capital invested in government securities. They also dominated Indochinese trade: in 1938 53 per cent of Indochina's exports went to France. Between 1931 and 1938 Indochina's imports from France averaged 57 per cent of its total imports.[5]

Despite the economic impact of French rule the economy of Vietnam remained predominantly agrarian. Even in 1940 the peasants still constituted between 85 and 90 per cent of the population. Changes were, however, taking place, particularly in the system of land ownership. They were especially marked in Cochinchina where the extension of rice cultivation and rubber plantations put large estates in the hands of a small landed class with control of 80 per cent of the rice-fields, where some 200,000 families were employed in sharecropping. Sharecroppers commonly paid the landlord 40 per cent of the crop, in addition to furnishing various gifts and services – a practice reminiscent of some feudal system. Furthermore, tenants were obliged to pay exorbitant interest on their landlord's capital and for any credit advanced by him. Peasants who had a small holding of their own were also forced to pay huge sums in interest – up to 120 per cent per annum – to moneylenders. All peasants suffered additionally from high taxation imposed by the government, which also operated a monopoly on the purchase and distribution of alcohol, opium and salt, thus removing from the villages their secondary means of livelihood.[6]

Village communities were weakened in other ways: when, for instance, village notables were made to relinquish their authority to officials trained by the French. Deprived of their natural leaders, those communities became more vulnerable to outside pressures. Much of their land fell into the hands of mandarins who had chosen to help both the French and themselves. As communal life was disrupted and population increases accentuated the scarcity of land, the villages lost more of their members to new urban centres and industrial enterprises such as rubber plantations. Although villages continued to be the focus of life in the countryside, they were less able to hold their communities together and they had lost much of their former autonomy.

French rule created a new societal structure in Vietnam. Those who benefited from the colonial dispensation included the large landowners and a small, mainly foreign, upper class of capitalists. There also emerged, as a result of economic developments, a small middle class. At the bottom of the pyramid were those exploited by the first groups: the landless tenants and an emergent working class composed of miners, plantation workers, public works employees and industrial labourers. Somewhat apart from the other groups was a comparatively large intelligentsia – a disillusioned élite, ready to provide recruits for factions opposed to the colonial regime.[7]

It is worth noting here that the nature of opposition to French rule altered significantly over the years. The French had imposed a new kind of domination whose overthrow required new forms of national awareness and different modes of political action.[8] What began as a struggle to reinstate the old Confucian system was transformed into a demand for drastic changes within Vietnamese society. Conflict developed not only between the nationalists and the French but also among the nationalists themselves. Traditionalists opposed those who sought to restructure society. Within the ranks of the reformers there was a division between advocates of change by constitutional means and others who worked for a revolution.

During the first decades of the French regime there was a series of revolts led by those mandarins who, having refused to collaborate with the conquerors, were determined to restore the old system. The most notable was the so-called Scholars' Revolt of 1885, an attempt to seize power in the name of the young emperor Ham Nghi.[9] Inspired by the moral authority of the scholars and mandarins who led the revolt, the peasants rallied to the cause. Their struggle persisted for three years, impressing even the French by its tenacity. Finally, in 1888, Ham Nghi was captured, after many of his followers had been killed in battle or succumbed to disease. The brutality of the colonial troops in putting down the revolt helped to provoke more mandarin-led-uprisings in the course of the next ten years. Such localized efforts to turn back the clock were suppressed with increasing severity and by 1900 the traditionalists had virtually shot their bolt. Every defeat they suffered was a reminder that the old monarchy was incapable of providing effective resistance to the foreigners, who enjoyed modern weapons and superior organization. How could a dynasty which had lost the country its independence and then had failed to restore it, claim that it had the mandate of heaven? Many concluded that it could not and new resistance movements emerged with aims other than the re-establishment of the traditional monarchy.

One man who epitomized the new nationalism was Phan Boi Chau.[10] He argued that, in order to overthrow the French, it was necessary to learn from them. Vietnamese society must, he felt, be modernized before it could regain its independence. In 1905 he visited Japan, whose Meiji emperors had, as a result of westernization, been able to create a formidable military power. During the Russo–Japanese war Japan had imposed a humiliating defeat on the Russian empire which undermined the myth of white supremacy and inspired nationalist movements throughout Asia.[11] Chau believed that Vietnam should follow the Japanese example. Accordingly he founded a Reform Association to win freedom under the leadership of a reformed monarchy. In 1908 it supported a popular protest in Central Vietnam against high taxation and corvée labour.[12] It was the first anti–French demonstration by peasants demanding redress of specific grievances. However, neither Chau nor his lieutenants fully appreciated at that stage the potential of peasant movements. The French easily put down the rebellion and arrested most of its leaders. Chau himself fled to Japan.

Some years later, in 1911, a revolution in China overthrew the Manchu dynasty and Chau, who had previously been impressed by its prime mover, Sun Yat-sen, made his way to Canton. Dazzled by the success of Sun's Kuomintang (Nationalist) party, Chau abandoned his schemes for a reformed and reforming monarchy and established, in 1912, the Viet-Nam Phuc-Quoc Hoi (Vietnamese Independence Association) with the aim of creating a democratic republic in Vietnam. From his base at Canton Chau was, for more than a decade, 'the most determined and radical Vietnamese agitator and the most effective political educator, the man the French regarded as the most dangerous nationalist revolutionary . . .'[13] He was the instigator of several uprisings and numerous insurrectionary incidents until his career as a revolutionary ended in 1925 with his arrest by the French.

Although Phan Boi Chau had, for a quarter of a century, caused the French a great deal of trouble, they were in 1925 still firmly ensconced in Vietnam and apparently able to cope with all attempts to remove them. Chau, for all his zeal, had serious weaknesses. His talent as an agitator was flawed by an inability to expound effectively the purpose of his revolutionary activity. The modernization of Vietnam was an unhelpfully vague goal and Chau neglected to provide a practical programme of specific political and economic demands. Nor did he make productive contact with the mass of Vietnamese, the peasants. He concentrated his effort on the élite and tended to count on outside help rather than on decisive action from the Vietnamese themselves.

1. Ai Quoc (Ho Chi Minh) reads the declaration of independence of the provisional government, September 1945.

Shortly before Chau was arrested a Vietnamese nationalist of a different stamp arrived in Canton. Nguyen Ai Quoc had been sent by the Communist International to join a mission, led by Michael Borodin, whose task was to aid Sun Yat-sen in organizing the Kuomintang. Ai Quoc's main concern, however, was not to strengthen the nationalist movement in China, but to create an effective revolutionary force in Vietnam. For nearly half a century he was to play a major role in Vietnamese politics. In the period between the wars he was the inspirer of a new brand of revolutionaries. After the Second World War he became the dominant figure in his own country and achieved world-wide fame under the name he adopted in 1942 – Ho Chi Minh.[14]

Ho was born with the name Nguyen Sinh Cung in 1890 in Nghe An, a province noted for the rebelliousness of its inhabitants. From his father and his environment he acquired a hatred of French imperialism and a strong sense of patriotism. In 1911 he left Vietnam as a cabin boy and spent two years at sea. During that time he visited a number of countries and became increasingly concerned with politics – in particular with the plight of his native land. In 1917 he made his way to Paris where he built up contacts with the numerous Vietnamese who, in the course of the First World War, had been sent to France. He became their spokesman and recruited their services for the struggle to gain recognition and betterment for Vietnam. (It was at this time that he adopted the name Ai Quoc, the patriot.) In 1919 he drew up a programme for the emancipation of his country which included requests for permanent representation in the French parliament, freedom of the press, an amnesty for political prisoners and equality of legal rights between French and Vietnamese. The programme was forwarded to the secretariat of the Paris Peace Conference, then attempting to settle the affairs of the world after the end of the war, but was not discussed. Clemenceau Lloyd George and Wilson, the men who dominated the conference, were selective in their anti-imperialism. While they enthusiastically dismembered the empires of Germany and Austro–Hungary, they preserved and even extended their own. Communism rather than imperialism was their enemy.

It was to the communists that Ai Quoc turned for support. At the Eighteenth Congress of the French Socialist Party, held in December 1920, he inveighed against the 'abhorrent crimes' committed by imperialists against his native land and voted in favour of joining the Third International. Founded in Moscow in 1919, the Third (Communist) International was dedicated to the expansion of communism as an international movement. Its moving spirit was Lenin, whose writings had turned Ai Quoc into a dedicated revolutionary.

Many years later he explained that at first he had respected Lenin 'purely because he was a great patriot who had set his countrymen free'.[15] Subsequently he was deeply impressed by Lenin's theses on the problem of nationalities and the colonial peoples. 'My joy was so great,' he commented, 'that at times I was reduced to tears. Alone in my room, I would cry out as though standing before a great crowd: "My beloved, downtrodden, luckless compatriots! This is what we need, this is our road to freedom!"'[16] In the first place it was patriotism, not communism, that led him to believe in Lenin and the Third International. Eventually, after studying Marxism–Leninism and involving himself in practical work, he became convinced that only communism was 'capable of bringing freedom to the oppressed and to working people all over the world'.[17]

In 1923 Ai Quoc was sent to Moscow as the French Communist Party delegate to the Peasant International. He remained to study communism and, in 1924, to attend the Fifth Congress of the Comintern. Thereafter, as already noted, he joined Borodin in Canton where he began to organize an Indochinese communist movement. In February 1930 he persuaded three competing communist groups to unite to form the Vietnamese Communist Party which, to emphasize its international character, renamed itself in October the Indochinese Communist Party (Dong Duong Cong San Dong).[18] The newly united party was soon put to the test by a major rising of the peasants in Nghe An province.

Open rebellion occurred in northern Annam during the summer of 1930, when famine was added to the other miseries of the people. Consequently the communist party succeeded in activating not only the peasants but also factory workers in the provinces of Nghe An and Ha Tinh. The main force was provided by the peasantry, six thousand of whom staged a hunger march on 12 September to the town of Vinh. The colonial administration was totally disrupted and replaced by local councils called xo-viets. These Vietnamese soviets managed to survive for several months, instituting a programme of reforms which allowed the communists to claim that the revolution had been put into effect. Their success was however short-lived; early in 1931 the French assembled enough troops to take the offensive. The repression that followed demonstrated the ferocity of an imperial power when it felt threatened. It is estimated that 10,000 Vietnamese were killed and 50,000 deported. Buttinger has commented: 'People were killed not in the heat of battle – there were no battles – but rather they were chased, hunted down, and murdered by a soldiery drunk on blood.'[19]

The scale of the Nghe An rebellion contrasted significantly with an uprising organized by the Vietnamese Nationalist Party (Vietnam Quoc Dan Dang). Founded three years previously it modelled itself on the Kuomintang in China, seeking to replace French dominion with a republican government on the lines of the regime led by Chiang Kai-shek. In February its leaders staged a mutiny of the Vietnamese garrison troops at Yen-Bay in Tonkin which was intended to initiate a chain reaction of incidents culminating in a full-scale revolution. Owing to faulty organization and poor security the French had no difficulty in suppressing the uprising at its inception. The Nationalist leaders were executed and the party itself never recovered. Henceforth revolutionary movements in Tonkin were dominated by the communists.[20]

Despite the setbacks caused by the white terror of 1931, Nguyen Ai Quoc was greatly encouraged by the events of the previous year. The unified communist movement in Indochina had gained a psychological victory with the Nghe An revolution. While the terrorist methods of the Nationalist Party had proved wholly ineffective, the setting up of the soviets in Annam and their capacity to organize a mass movement had convinced many peasants that a successful revolution was possible. The French, it appeared, could be ousted if only the rural population were mobilized on the side of an armed independence movement.

Even so, nearly a quarter of a century elapsed before the French were finally forced from Vietnam, their withdrawal being precipitated by events outwith the control of the Vietnamese nationalists. In 1939 the French declared war on Nazi Germany. Within a year they were forced to capitulate and were powerless to prevent Hitler's ally, Japan, from assuming control of their empire in Indochina. It was only during the Japanese occupation that an effective nationalist movement at last emerged.

The nature of that movement had been determined by the lessons learned in the period between the two world wars. During those years it became evident that the gradualist approach of those who sought independence by constitutional means could not succeed. The constitutionalists were an urban élite who failed to find any significant following in the countryside.[21] While they were prepared to work within the system created by the colonial power, the support of the rural masses was being won by those who appreciated that the system could not be manipulated; that it must be destroyed. It was evident that the French had no intention of sharing power in any foreseeable future. Such Vietnamese participation as did exist, for example in Cochinchina, was spurious: it stopped well short of the point at which decisions were made.

In fact the French ruled by coercion, not through consultation. The situation therefore demanded a conspiratorial rather than a constitutional opposition. To survive in a police-state it was essential to create the kind of underground network at which the communists excelled. Another aspect of French rule which the communists turned to their own advantage was the economic policy. Its blatant exploitation of the Vietnamese economy provided a most telling confirmation of the Leninist critique of imperialism. As one historian has observed, the subordination of Vietnam to French economic interests was for young Vietnamese 'a classic example of the imperialist state's treatment of a colony. It was Viet-Nam's fate, or less dramatically its historical experience, that Marxist ideals should have appealed to men who proved themselves to be the best organized and the best able to lead.'[22]

The Vietnamese masses meanwhile knew nothing of Marx. Their hatred of the French derived from the misery of their lives and a deeply rooted national consciousness. Foreign dogma had little appeal to men who revered above all their land and their ancestors. The leaders of the communist party realized however that without the backing of the peasants there would be no socialist revolution. Marx himself had dismissed the peasants as mere beasts of burden and Stalin, the voice of world communism, considered that the vanguard of the revolution must be drawn from the urban workers. Nguyen Ai Quoc, more a man of action than an armchair theorist,[23] was convinced that, regardless of orthodox Marxist opinion, the peasants could make excellent recruits to the cause of revolution. The Nghe An experience had shown what could be achieved. The next stage was to raise the revolutionary consciousness of peasants throughout Vietnam. Ten years after Nghe An the disruption caused by the Second World War gave Ai Quoc his chance.

Two

THE WAR AGAINST THE FRENCH
1946–54

The fall of France in 1940 was followed by the establishment of the pro-Nazi Vichy government, a collaborationist regime with Marshal Pétain at its head. Supporters of Pétain also assumed control of the French administration in Indochina, where they co-operated fully with the Japanese in their campaigns against the Vietnamese nationalists. As a result of the Nazi–Soviet Pact[1] the communists in Vietnam were at first under orders not to oppose the Japanese. In 1941 they were extricated from that invidious position when Hitler invaded the Soviet Union. Thereafter both Germany and Japan were officially recognized as imperialist aggressors. Even before Stalin's enforced volte-face Nguyen Ai Quoc had founded, in May 1941, the League for Vietnamese Independence (Vietnam Doc Lap Dong Minh), soon to become famous as the Vietminh.

Although it was set up at a meeting of the central committee of the Indochinese Communist Party, the Vietminh was intended to attract support not only from communists but from all shades of nationalist opinion. In June 1941 it made the following appeal; 'Rich people, soldiers, workers, peasants, intellectuals, employees, traders, youth and women who warmly love your country! At the present time national liberation is the most important problem. Let us unite together!'[2] The genuineness of that appeal has been a matter of some debate. Certain historians have argued that the Vietminh was essentially a nationalist movement with its emphasis on 'the country's history, the Flag, Vietnamese culture . . .'[3] Others have contended that it was merely a cover for the communists; that while it posed as a union of patriots, in fact it was 'hiding its real ideological nature until such time as independence had been won'.[4] The issue has often been put in a more personal way. Was Ho Chi Minh in essence a nationalist whose communism was more a means than an end? Alternatively, was he a communist above all, who found it convenient to masquerade as a nationalist? Such questions are best considered after we have examined the history of the Vietminh. At this point we might note that Ho considered such a dichotomy pointless. He saw himself as both a nationalist and a communist, the one role complementing the other.[5]

His problem, after the founding of the Vietminh, was not, however, to scrutinize his own motives but to gain the maximum support for his new organization. China, Vietnam's northern neighbour, was the nearest source of aid. Since 1936 there had been in China an alliance, albeit uneasy, between the communists and the Kuomintang in order to defeat the Japanese, who had launched a full-scale invasion of the country in 1937. In order to make contact with both groups Ho crossed into China in July 1942 and was promptly arrested by the Kuomintang. He spent the next fifteen months in shackles, hustled from jail to jail, covered with scabies and half-starved. Eventually he was released, when his captors realized that he might be of some use to them. At that stage of the Second World War Chiang Kai-shek, the head of the Kuomintang, had the firm support of the allied leaders and was expected to remain as the dominant figure in China when the Japanese were defeated. It was even proposed that he might assume control of the northern part of Vietnam. With that prospect in mind, the Kuomintang were anxious to win over local support and in October 1942 established the Vietnam Revolutionary Alliance (Dong Min Hoi). They were soon forced to realize that without the support of the Vietminh the alliance would make little headway. Accordingly, Ho Chi Minh was released and made leader of the Dong Min Hoi! The nationalist cause in Vietnam was thus reinforced by the very people who thought they were undermining it. Its outstanding leader gained not only his freedom but also the co-operation of the Kuomintang, who clearly underestimated his talents as a dissembler.

During the next two years the Vietminh provided the main resistance to the Japanese and gained the sympathy and admiration of American military intelligence officers who fought at their side. One of the US leaders in the field advised his superiors: 'Forget the communist bogy. VML [the Vietminh League] is not communist, stands for freedom and reforms from French harshness. If French go part way with them they might work with French.'[6] Later reports described Ho as a 'brilliant and capable man' and commented that his troops 'made up . . . in spirit what they lacked in training'.[7] With American support Ho established a strategic base-area in the Cao-Bang province of Vietnam and was fully prepared to take advantage of two crucial events in the final stage of the war in Asia.

The first was the *coup d'état* in Vietnam by the Japanese on 9 March 1945. Within twenty-four hours the Japanese army disarmed and imprisoned French military units in Indochina. At the same time all French officials were dismissed and many interned. Now that the war was clearly going against them the Japanese no longer trusted their former collaborators. In supplanting them they put an end, for the time being, to French influence in Vietnam. Before the coup the Vietminh had two enemies to contend with; after it only the Japanese stood between them and independence, but not for long. On 6 August 1945 the Japanese city of Hiroshima was totally destroyed by one atomic bomb. Three days later a second bomb devastated Nagasaki and the Japanese government quickly sued for peace. On 13 August the Vietminh formed a National Liberation Committee; within a week they controlled Hanoi and became in effect a provisional government. Bao Dai, the puppet emperor of Vietnam under the Japanese, abdicated and on 2 September in Hanoi, Ho Chi Minh, his beard blowing about and his voice heavy with emotion, proclaimed his country's independence.[8]

The Declaration of Independence of the Democratic Republic of Vietnam began, ironically enough in the light of later events, with a quotation from the American Declaration of Independence of 1776: 'All men are created equal. They are endowed by their Creator with certain inalienable rights, among these are Life, Liberty and the pursuit of Happiness.' It went on to describe how the French had denied such rights to the Vietnamese: '. . . they have deprived our people of every democratic liberty . . . They have enforced inhuman laws . . . They have built more prisons than schools . . . they have drowned our uprisings in rivers of blood . . . They have fleeced us to the backbone, impoverished our people and devastated our land . . . They have hampered the prospering of our national bourgeoisie; they have mercilessly exploited our workers.' Having condemned past misdeeds, it then anticipated a better future: '. . . we, members of the Provincial Government, representing the whole Vietnamese people, declare that from now on we break off all relations of a colonial character with France . . . The whole Vietnamese people, animated by a common purpose, are determined to fight to the bitter end against any attempt by the French colonialists to reconquer their country.'[9]

Their declaration of independence was made at the end of a war ostensibly on behalf of democracy and the Vietnamese hoped for powerful support against any French move to reimpose colonial rule. They were convinced, they said, that the Allied nations would not refuse to acknowledge the independence of a people who had fought with them against the fascists. Vietnam had the right to be free and independent and, they affirmed, was so already. The blunt statement that Vietnam had already gained its independence was, in a sense, true. As we have seen, Ho Chi Minh had established a government in the north. At the same time a People's Committee was set up in Saigon under Tran Van Giau, the communist leader of the southern Vietminh. The French historian Devillers has recorded that 'ten days after the Japanese capitulation, the Vietminh controlled the entire territory of Vietnam'.[10] Meanwhile France itself was in a desperate plight. The ravages of war had turned the whole country upside down and the prospect of the French regaining control of their former empire in Indochina seemed remote.

Given that Vietnam was *de facto* an ex-colony, its government might have been organized under a trusteeship, as had been suggested by the American President, Roosevelt. He was highly critical of the French colonial record and believed that the people of Indochina deserved something better. His prescription was a trusteeship exercised by the great powers who would supervise the progressive development of the Vietnamese towards self-government. At the Yalta Conference of February 1945 the proposal had a mixed reception. According to Roosevelt, while the Soviets and the Chinese were agreeable, the British opposed it, fearing that it might break up their empire: 'if the Indo–Chinese were to work together and eventually get their independence the Burmese might do the same thing.'[11]

Roosevelt had no chance to modify the British attitude since he died in April 1945. At the next meeting of the great powers, held at Potsdam in July and August, America was represented by a new president, Truman, who was concerned less about French colonialism than about Soviet imperialism. In his opinion, liberating the Vietnamese from the French was a secondary issue. The big question was how to contain the Soviet Union. He accepted the need for some changes in Vietnam, but only under the auspices of the French. There was to be no trusteeship in Indochina except under the French government, which would be asked 'at some appropriate time' to say what its intentions were regarding basic liberties and some movement towards self-determination.[12]

Truman's policy shift pleased not only the French but also the British. They, no less than the French, had been humiliated by the Japanese in the early years of the war in the Pacific. Asian peoples had seen them driven from Hong Kong, Singapore and Burma. Even India, the jewel of the British Empire, had been menaced by the Japanese. The restoration of that empire to its former power was one of Churchill's main objectives in 1945. It could not be restored without holding in check the nationalist forces which had been encouraged by the defeats sustained by the white colonial powers. The British had long experience of dealing with nationalism and knew how contagious it was. Like Roosevelt, they realized that if Indochina broke away from France it would be so much harder to contain other Asian peoples within the British empire. Whatever Churchill's view of the French, he was bound to favour them against the Vietnamese.

To everyone's amazement, Churchill himself was not present at the second session of the Potsdam Conference. His unexpected electoral defeat resulted in a Labour government under Attlee who, unlike Churchill, had considerable sympathy for the nationalist movement in India. Indeed, within three years of his coming to power, both India and Burma gained their independence. However, at the time of the Potsdam Conference he had been in office only for a few weeks. It was hardly likely that in so short a time he would re-orientate British policy in Southeast Asia. The conference in fact confirmed that, pending a final settlement, Indochina should be divided at the sixteenth parallel. China was to control the northern part while the south came under the jurisdiction of Mountbatten, the British commander in the Pacific. His instructions were to take over the Japanese headquarters and disarm and repatriate their troops. In addition, he was to release and transport home allied prisoners-of-war. He was to occupy no more territory than was necessary to carry out his orders and was to withdraw his troops as soon as possible. A similar brief was given to the Chinese.

The Potsdam decision seriously weakened the position of the nationalists in Vietnam. For a time, admittedly brief, the Vietminh had been the only effective force in the country. The dreams of the revolutionaries seemed to have come true. Their enemies were defeated, their country united and their right to rule themselves was about to be confirmed by all the allies. However, far from recognizing their independence, the allies had superseded the authority of the Provisional Government by partitioning the country and occupying it with the armies of two of the major powers. We consider first the impact of the British in the south.

At first the nationalists expected co-operation from the British and arranged a friendly reception for General Gracey when he arrived in Saigon on 13 September 1945. The Vietminh decorated the route from the airport to the city with British, American and Vietminh flags and pro-allied slogans, one of which read 'Welcome to the Allies, to the British and the Americans, but we have no room for the French.'[13] Very quickly, however, the British outlived their welcome. Although the Vietminh had assumed control of Saigon and, given the circumstances, were running a fairly efficient administration, Gracey refused to have any dealings with them. He had no doubt that the French were entitled to restore their empire and that it was, therefore, pointless to recognize the nationalists.

Fearful that their influence was being eroded the Vietminh organized boycotts and demonstrations against the British. Gracey retaliated by closing their newspapers and enforcing martial law. On 23 September he permitted a group of French troops and civilians, whom he had armed the previous day, to seize the Vietminh headquarters. Most of them had been prisoners of the Vietminh since the surrender of Japan and were determined to take revenge for their former humiliations, which they did with excessive brutality. Even the most moderate Vietnamese were alienated by the shootings and beatings that followed: people who had once been willing to negotiate terms, 'after being gun-whipped and thrown into jail emerged as bitter opponents of French rule'.[14]

As usual, violence begat violence. On 25 September European and Eurasian civilians were massacred in the Cité Hérodia, a suburb of Saigon; estimates of the dead vary from 150 to 300. The massacre was probably the work of the Binh Xuyen, thugs from the Saigon underworld. Nevertheless, the Vietminh were held responsible and Gracey decided to crush them. In the war that followed he relied heavily on the Japanese troops in the area, thus reducing the casualties of his own British and Indian soldiers. MacArthur, the American commander in the Pacific, declared: 'If there is anything that makes my blood boil, it is to see our allies in Indo-China . . . deploying Japanese troops to reconquer these little people we promised to liberate. It is the most ignoble kind of betrayal.'[15] In January 1946 Nehru, one of the leaders of the nationalist movement in India, told the *New York Times*: 'We have watched British intervention . . . with growing anger, shame and helplessness, that Indian troops should be used for doing Britain's dirty work against our friends who are fighting the same fight as we.'[16]

Nehru's protest was made when the issue was apparently settled. By early 1946 Gracey's forces had destroyed, at least temporarily, nationalist resistance in the south of Vietnam. Their victory was the object of some criticism even in Britain. Laski, an influential figure in the Labour Party, believed that the intervention in Indochina made 'the British claim to have been engaged in a war for democracy and freedom seem a hollow mockery all over South-East Asia'.[17] Outlining the official attitude, Bevin, the Foreign Secretary, explained that the government did not wish to be involved in the affairs of non-British territories. Therefore it had expedited the movement of French troops to Saigon to enable them to relieve the British.[18] From the outset it had assumed that the French should be re-established in Indochina. In the light of subsequent developments we might feel that the British policy was disastrously mistaken. It would, however, have been a remarkably bold move to stand in the way of the French. What, we might consider, would have been the reaction in France, and in the USA, if the British had favoured the Vietminh? What grounds were there for believing that the nationalists in the south were capable of sustaining a stable administration? Was it realistic to expect a new and inexperienced government to effect a reversal of policy which would have caused repercussions throughout the whole of Asia, including a major upheaval in India?

Discounting such considerations, Rosie has argued that British actions set the scene for a prolonged confrontation. He claims that the British force destroyed a genuinely popular revolution and put down the risings which followed. Had it not done so the French would probably have been obliged to come to terms with the nationalists. If, he asks, 'the French had been forced to assume a moderate position in 1945, would the world have seen the protracted Franco–Vietminh war of 1946–54 and the American–Vietnamese war of today?'[19]

There is no doubt that the re-imposition of French control in the south strengthened their standing throughout the country. Even so, under Ho Chi Minh, the Vietminh in the north had begun a programme of action which gained them considerable public confidence. Ho was confident enough himself to organize general elections which were held in January 1946, not only in northern and central Indochina but also secretly in numerous parts of the French zone in the south. The results, which gave the Vietminh a clear majority in the assembly, were, according to one authority, 'probably fairly indicative of the state of public opinion at that time'.[20] The new government won further support through the effectiveness of its campaign to produce more food when its people were threatened with starvation, a common occurrence in Southeast Asia. In the words of the American historian, Ellen Hammer: 'when the Spring of 1946 came, the people did not starve. Conditions were still not good, but the VietMinh had succeeded in doing what the French had not always been able to do: they had saved the country from famine by the unaided efforts of their citizens.'[21]

Although his government had proved the viability of self-determination, and while some of his supporters demanded a total break with the colonial past, Ho Chi Minh was prepared to negotiate with the French. He appreciated the possible advantages of co-operation with France and was also apprehensive about the influence of the Chinese, who, under the terms of Potsdam, had an army of between 150,000 and 185,000 men in occupation of northern Indochina. For twenty years the Kuomintang had been in conflict with their indigenous communists; it was hardly likely that they would look favourably on a communist-dominated administration in Hanoi. Bearing in mind the clash of ideologies and the long memory of Chinese intervention in Vietnam, Ho's apprehension seemed to be well founded. 'It is better,' he is reported as saying, 'to sniff France's dung for a while than eat China's all our lives.'[22] In fact the Chinese Nationalists did not aim to stay permanently in Vietnam. Their main concern was to strengthen their hold in China itself against the encroachments of the communists. Thus, in February 1946, they recognized French sovereignty over Indochina. At the same time the French surrendered their territorial and economic privileges in China. The Franco–Chinese settlement exerted pressure on Ho Chi Minh to come to terms with the French, whose 'rights' in Vietnam had been endorsed by both occupying powers.

On 6 March 1946 Ho's government agreed to give the French a friendly reception when they relieved the Chinese troops. In return the French recognized the republic of Vietnam as a free state, with a government, a parliament, and an army: a state which formed part of the Indochinese Federation and the French Union. This supposed settlement in fact settled nothing, being 'little more than an armistice that provided a transient illusion of agreement where no agreement actually existed'.[23] Giap, later to become the outstanding Vietminh general, compared it to the Brest–Litovsk treaty the Bolsheviks had made with the German High Command in 1918. It was a humiliation to be endured in order to give the Vietminh time to create an effective fighting force and should be repudiated as soon as possible.[24] The powerful colonial lobby in France looked on the agreement with equal distaste. For them also it was a means of buying time while they consolidated their forces in the south. Both Ho and the more moderate leaders in France came under attack from their own sides.

Ho's visit to France in June 1946 did little to improve matters. Even before he reached Paris, d'Argenlieu[25] had set up a so-called 'autonomous republic' in Cochinchina: an obvious device for dividing Vietnam while the French manoeuvred to regain control of the whole country for themselves. With the conflict between the extreme nationalists and the neo-colonialists becoming increasingly bitter there was a desperate need for some moderator; but none appeared. It was only one year since the end of the Second World War and the great powers had more urgent problems to deal with. They were, in any case, divided themselves. The alliance created by the struggle against Germany and Japan disintegrated as the Cold War ensued. Furthermore, the major issue in the Far East was not the fate of Vietnam but the conflict between the Kuomintang and the communists in China.

In September 1946 Ho Chi Minh made a further agreement with the French which did little more than recapitulate the ineffectual settlement of the previous March. But the time for compromise was running out. France was passing through a constitutional crisis: disgusted with the old Third Republic, the French were seeking an alternative form of government. While they were preoccupied with founding the Fourth Republic, the conduct of affairs in Vietnam was left to the most uncompromising enemies of the nationalist movement. The Vietminh responded to the intransigence of the *colons* with acts of terrorism. Towards the end of November the French retaliated by shelling the port of Haiphong from the cruiser *Suffren*. Six thousand Vietnamese were killed and with them died the remote possibility of a peaceful solution. Within a month Ho was exhorting his countrymen to rise against the French: 'Let him who has a rifle use his rifle, let him who has a sword use his sword! And let those who have no sword take up pick-axes and sticks.'[26]

The *colons*, seriously underestimating the strength of an enemy whom they dismissed contemptuously as 'les jaunes', expected an easy victory over the Vietminh. After a year of fighting the French Minister of War felt able to announce that 'there was no longer any military problem in Indo-China'.[27] At the same time the *Journal de Saigon* claimed that Ho Chi Minh represented 'nothing at all'.[28] As the war dragged on, the French were forced to admit that the Vietminh did have considerable support and that the military problem was persisting. Accordingly they tried to weaken the Vietminh by establishing another Vietnamese regime. On 14 June 1949, Bao Dai was proclaimed head of the 'new' state of Vietnam. This French manoeuvre to solve an intractable military problem with a political device failed. Bao Dai's only hope of attracting people away from the Vietminh was to make himself credible as an independent leader. It was obvious, however, that he owed his position to the French. His government was made up of nonentities – no one of national reputation would serve under him.

On the other hand, their campaign against the French had toughened the morale of the Vietminh and enhanced the authority of Ho Chi Minh. Suffering economic and financial strain, the French were embroiled in a war against a resourceful enemy, while their potential allies simply looked on. Although the American government was apprehensive about the Vietminh's communist affiliations, it was not prepared to intervene. Even after Bao Dai was offered as a non-communist alternative to Ho the State Department declared: 'We cannot at this time irretrievably commit the US to support of a native government which . . . might become virtually a puppet government separated from the people and existing only by the presence of French military forces.'[29]

The situation changed dramatically when, in October 1949, the Chinese Communists finally ousted the Nationalists and set up their own government. In December their troops reached the northern border of Vietnam. On the thirtieth of that month President Truman approved a National Security Council study on Asia which recommended that the USA provide 'political, economic and military assistance and advice' to areas threatened by communist aggression. It suggested that 'particular attention should be given to the problem of French Indochina'. In February 1950 the French made a request for military aid which was sympathetically received by Acheson, the US Secretary of State. He warned Truman that if America failed to support the 'legal governments in Indochina' it would 'face the extension of Communism over the remainder of the continental area of South-east Asia and possibly westward'.[30] The American government announced in May that it would make the French an initial grant of \$10 million.[31] Objectively the conflict in Vietnam may have seemed much as before: communist-led nationalists trying to unseat the French. Viewed from Washington, however, the war had become part of the free world's struggle against international communism.

It is important to consider why the US became at this point 'directly involved in the developing tragedy in Vietnam'. What persuaded them that a localized colonial war fitted into the pattern of a world-wide communist conspiracy? Early in 1950 the communist government in China had given diplomatic recognition to the Democratic Republic of Vietnam; on 31 January the Soviet Union followed suit. That recognition, said Acheson, 'should remove any illusions as to the "nationalist" character of Ho Chi Minh's aims and reveals Ho in his true colours as the mortal enemy of native independence in Indochina'.[32] Acheson's statement betrays the Cold War psychosis that was then affecting American policy.

There can be little doubt that Ho Chi Minh wanted, above all, to achieve independence for Vietnam; it was the cause to which he had devoted his whole life. What he sought from his fellow-communists in Moscow and Peking was recognition, not domination. The Vietminh had made their own revolution in 1945 and since then had fought alone against the French. There was no reason for making themselves pawns of Mao or Stalin. Nor was there any evidence that they had done so. There was ample evidence, however, that the American leaders had been badly shaken by the defection, as they saw it, of China to the communist camp. What impelled them to help the French was not so much the absurd assumption that Ho Chi Minh had become a Soviet puppet, but rather the stark fact that Mao Tse-tung controlled China. Disturbed by the implications of that fact, the US over-reacted and saw China as a greater menace that it was. Having discarded the illusion that the Chinese Nationalists could hold China, they then deluded themselves that the Communist Chinese were poised to seize the whole of South-east Asia. This led to the conviction that the Vietminh were not genuine nationalists but merely a communist fifth-column. It became imperative therefore to support the French anti-communist crusade. The outbreak of war in Korea, in June 1950, made them even more determined to maintain French control of Indochina.

2. General Vo Nguyen Giap with a young anti-aircraft gunner.

However, despite American financial and other support, the French made little headway against the Vietminh. To explain their failure we must look beyond the purely military aspect of the war. Not everyone saw it as an anti-communist crusade. Many Frenchmen still felt that it was a colonial war which was becoming more difficult to justify as nationalist movements elsewhere were being recognized by former colonial powers. The British, for example had retired from India and Burma. The Dutch had been obliged to concede self-rule to their East Indian possessions. While a swift victory in Indochina might have been recognized as an accomplished fact, a protracted and inconclusive struggle was becoming unacceptable. General Giap's estimation of the war was proving to be correct. 'The enemy', he had predicted, 'will pass slowly from the offensive to the defensive. The blitzkreig will transform itself into a war of long duration. Thus, the enemy will be caught in a dilemma – he has to drag out the war in order to win it and does not possess, on the other hand, the psychological and political means to fight a long drawn out war.'[33]

By 1954 such means were virtually exhausted. Although the USA was already bearing nearly 80 per cent of the cost of the war effort, the French needed even more help to avoid defeat. Having sustained some 90,000 casualties during more than seven years of guerrilla warfare, they determined, in the spring of 1954, on a major confrontation with the Vietminh at Dienbienphu.[34] French military leaders imagined that Giap's primitive supply system would be inadequate to provide the resources for a pitched battle, and expected that his irregulars would be overwhelmed by their own professional troops. It was a disastrous miscalculation. The Vietminh did in fact concentrate enough men and materials, including artillery, to take on the French. Dienbienphu was besieged and its garrison decimated by artillery bombardment and human-wave attacks. At the end of March its airfield was destroyed. Thereafter the garrison's only hope was the breakthrough of a relieving force from Hanoi or Laos, 'a hopeless concept in view of the terrain and distances involved', or the destruction of the Vietminh by massive aerial bombardment.[35] At the beginning of April the French requested immediate intervention by American carrier-based aircraft to save the day.

While Dulles, the Secretary of State, and Radford, Chairman of the Joint Chiefs of Staff, strongly favoured intervening, other

3. French soldiers dug in at Dienbienphu.

US service chiefs were more cautious. It was finally decided that America should not move on its own. Dulles had to inform the French that, while the American government was 'doing everything possible . . . to prepare [a] public, Congressional and Constitutional basis for united action', such action was not possible without 'active British Commonwealth participation'.[36] At Geneva, where an international conference on Korea and Indochina opened in April, Dulles canvassed British support. Eden, the British Foreign Secretary, promised to examine the situation afresh if the conference failed, but declined to take part in armed intervention at that juncture. While understanding American reluctance to act unilaterally, Bidault, the Foreign Minister of France, warned his allies that it was in fact too late to form a coalition since the fate of Indochina would be settled very shortly at Dienbienphu.[37]

The Vietminh did indeed overwhelm the remnants of the garrison on 7 May, a victory whose timing gave it the maximum political effect: the Indochina phase of the Geneva Conference began on the following day.

Three

THE FAILURE OF THE GENEVA SETTLEMENT: THE RULE OF NGO DINH DIEM IN THE SOUTH

The Geneva Conference was convened because the Vietminh could not be defeated. Had there been any hope of a military victory, the French would have rejected negotiation. The fact that they had been forced to the conference table shocked not only the French but also their friends in Britain and America. While French armies floundered in Vietnam, the British had suppressed a communist movement in Malaya and the Americans had supervised the defeat of a left-wing revolution in the Philippines.[1] After the collapse of the Geneva settlement, counter-insurgency techniques which had succeeded in those countries were employed in Vietnam, where they failed. Before we consider the terms of the settlement it is worth examining why Vietnam proved to be a special case.

The insurgency in Malaya (1948–54) was instigated by the Malayan Communist Party which, despite its name, was almost wholly Chinese in composition. (About 50 per cent of the population was Malay, the rest being mainly Indian and Chinese.) By the early 1950s some 8,000 armed communists were pitted against a much larger force of regular soldiers, police and village 'Home Guards'. Although few in number the communists posed a serious threat to the existing system and extraordinary methods were required to defeat them. Nevertheless they suffered from two fundamental weaknesses. First, they began as a minority faction and failed to attract support from ethnically different groups in the population. Second, while their terrorist campaign was being waged the colonial power promised self-government in Malaya.

The Hukbalahap revolution (1946–54) in the Philippines was the continuation of a movement which had originated before the Second World War with the aim of attacking landlordism in central Luzon. During the war the Huks were the backbone of resistance to the Japanese and contributed substantially to their final defeat. Totally disillusioned thereafter with the corruption and reactionary ineptitude of the ruling clique, the Huks attempted to overthrow the government. For a time their guerrilla tactics proved quite effective against a poorly led and badly equipped Philippine army but from the end of 1950 their strength ebbed. There were two major reasons for their failure. In the first place, their influence was localized. While conditions in their heartland, Luzon, were particularly favourable for an anti-establishment revolution, they were not replicated elsewhere, although there were ample grounds for social unrest throughout the Philippines. Secondly, the Huks were attacking a government which was, at least on the surface, independent. (In practice the US played a dominant role in the political and economic life of the islands.)

Turning to Vietnam, we can see that the Vietminh did not suffer from the basic weaknesses of the Chinese in Malaya and the Hukbalahap. Unlike the Malayan communists the Vietminh were ethnically the same as the rest of the population and were able to attract mass support. (It is worth noting the difference also between the colonial policies of the British and the French.) Similar contrasts can be made about the situation in the Philippines: for example, unlike the Huks, the influence of the Vietminh was not localized. During the long course of the struggle in Vietnam various experts were to suggest that anti-insurgency lessons learned in Malaya and the Philippines could be applied in Indochina. However, despite certain similarities, there were significant differences among the three areas of revolt. Perhaps the most fundamental was that, in contrast with the Vietminh, 'neither the Huks nor Malaya's Chinese insurgents could convincingly claim the nationalist mantle'.[2]

The question of Vietnamese nationalism was of major concern to the members of the Geneva Conference and the demarcation of national boundaries one of their principal tasks. Both the US and the South Vietnamese governments consistently misrepresented the decisions taken about boundaries. In particular they claimed that Vietnam had been divided into two states. The truth was that the settlement provided for a temporary division of the country to allow passions to cool. Thereafter, the temporary dividing line was to disappear, leaving one Vietnamese state which would include territories both north and south of the seventeenth parallel. Thus Article 1 of the Agreement on the Cessation of Hostilities

stipulated a 'provisional military demarcation line'. The forces of the People's Army of Vietnam were to be regrouped north of the line and the forces of the French Union to the south. An interval, after the regrouping had taken place, would allow some of the scars of a long war to heal. Only then would the future of the whole country be decided. The Final Declaration, paragraph seven, stated: 'In order to ensure that sufficient progress in the restoration of peace has been made, and that all the necessary conditions obtain for free expression of the national will, general elections shall be held in July 1956, under the supervision of an international commission . . .'[3]

The balance of forces in Vietnam at the time of the settlement indicated that the Vietminh would, in due course, control the whole country. Their main strength lay in the north, where they had done most of their fighting. With the departure of the French, there was no rival to their authority and they were able to begin the task of post-war reconstruction immediately. Even in the south there were numerous Vietminh supporters. (At Geneva the Vietminh had renounced 20 per cent of the territory it controlled and more than a million and a half inhabitants.[4]) Furthermore the south had, in the course of the war, become a political jungle in which warlords, bandits, secret societies and religious sects were rending each other. Contemporary French observers considered that there was little prospect of an effective administration emerging from such chaos.[5]

Ho Chi Minh urged those unfortunate enough to live in the south to endure the present. As a life-long advocate of a united, independent Vietnam he did not like even the 'temporary' split. However, he recognized the need to settle for less than an immediate total victory. He warned, for example, against those who 'see the French yet do not see the Americans'.[6] He himself saw the Americans clearly enough and understood that the very magnitude of the Vietminh victory at Dienbienphu, together with the political confusion in the south, would make them all the more determined to intervene in Vietnam. On 15 July 1954 he told the Central Committee of the Lao Dong (Communist) Party: 'At this moment American imperialism, the principal enemy of the peoples of the world, is becoming the direct principal enemy of the peoples of Indo-China; that is why all our actions must be aimed at this one enemy.'[7]

4. The Geneva Conference 1954: Bulganin, Eisenhower, Faure and Eden.

For their part the Americans appreciated that their main enemy in Indochina was Ho himself. President Eisenhower recognized in his memoirs the extent of Ho's appeal to his compatriots. 'I have never', he stated, 'talked or corresponded with a person knowledgable in Indochinese affairs who did not agree that had elections been held as of the time of the fighting, possibly 80 per cent of the population would have voted for the communist Ho Chi Minh . . .'[8] Clearly the US could not lightly accept a situation where a communist leader had such enormous popular support. To maintain American interests in Southeast Asia it was necessary to act against the Vietminh and to ensure that, in so far as the Geneva settlement might favour them, it would not be enforced. Eden, chairman of the final session of the Geneva Conference, had expressed the hope that it might have helped to strengthen the forces working for peace. The American leaders, however, felt that more important than peace was the containment of communism; and in their view a Vietminh victory was simply a communist triumph. Thus, while Eden was making his optimistic valedictory a small group of Americans was already preparing to carry on the struggle against the Vietminh.

Under the leadership of Colonel Edward Lansdale – one of the US advisers who helped the Philippine authorities to put down the Huks – the Saigon Military Mission entered Vietnam on 1 June 1954. It was a self-styled 'cold war combat team' whose objective was to carry out para-military operations against the 'enemy' and to wage political-psychological warfare. While the French and the Vietminh made great efforts to observe the terms of the settlement, Lansdale's team, in his words, 'pitched in' to fulfil its 'work load'. That load included the following: an abortive attempt to destroy the presses of the largest printing establishment in North Vietnam; the successful contamination of the oil supply of the Hanoi bus company to cause the wreckage of bus engines; writing detailed notes about potential targets and even the compilation of a bogus almanac predicting disaster for the Vietminh and success for the south.[9]

The military mission was an early earnest of US intentions to undermine the Geneva accords. At the beginning of August 1954 the National Security Council declared that the settlement 'completed a major forward stride of Communism which might lead to the loss of Southeast Asia'.[10] The use of the word 'loss' reveals a good deal about US foreign policy. In 1950 Senator Joseph McCarthy launched his career with the charge that the Truman Administration had connived at the loss of China to the Reds. Such terminology was characteristic of cold war attitudes which posited a division of the world into 'communist' and 'free'. Nations which ceased to be fully committed to the 'free world', that is the system of alliances dominated by the USA, were lost to the other side. Truman had given wide currency to the notion of a dichotomy in his doctrine, enunciated in 1947. 'At the present moment in world history', he declared, 'nearly every nation must choose between alternative ways of life.' It was a choice between democracy and totalitarianism; the role of the United States being to help those who opted for democracy and to defend them against 'armed minorities' and 'outside pressures'. As may become clear, US policy makers tended to interpret the term 'democracy' rather loosely. Indeed, according to Walter Lippmann, the Truman Doctrine led America into 'subsidizing the reactionary forces of the world'.[11]

Eisenhower followed the Truman line when on 20 August 1954 he approved a National Security Council paper on American policy in the Far East. The US thereby undertook to provide military, economic and political support for the anti-communist regime of Ngo Dinh Diem in South Vietnam. In a formal sense the support was conditional: Eisenhower's offer made the proviso that Diem's government should give assurances about 'the standards of performance it would be able to maintain'.[12] In practice, however, American prestige had been committed to 'defending' South Vietnam and it would be hard for any president to end that commitment. The Americans found that they had to tolerate very low 'standards of performance' from Diem and his successors.

During his first year in office Diem's position was rather precarious. Conditions in South Vietnam were so chaotic that in December 1954 General Lawton Collins, Eisenhower's personal representative, recommended that US plans for assisting Southeast Asia be re-evaluated.[13] The situation became even more fraught for Diem when, in the spring of 1955, the Hoa Hao and Cao Dai sects united with the Binh Xuyen gangsters, who controlled Saigon's police, in order to overthrow him. Collins persuaded Dulles that Diem must go. Diem, however, had the support of Lansdale who, through judicious bribery, managed to buy off some of the opposition. Diem then confronted the Binh Xuyen with regular army units and the power of the sects was broken. Henceforth Diem had full American backing and emerged as the strong man who would create a viable anti-communist state in South Vietnam.

Ngo Dinh Diem was a member of an aristocratic and, as we shall see, numerous family. As a devout Roman Catholic he was a thoroughgoing opponent of communism. His religion and his politics made him popular with such influential men as Cardinal Spellman and Senator John F. Kennedy when he visited the United States in 1950. The connections made during that visit strengthened his bid for the leadership of South Vietnam four years later.[14] Once he consolidated his position in 1955 he enjoyed, for the next eight years the confidence of his American allies.

Without their support he would not have remained in power in 1955 and 1956. Only the threat of US intervention prevented the Vietminh overrunning the south after Diem had refused even to

5. President Ngo Dinh Diem.

discuss the elections which, according to the Geneva settlement, were to be held in 1956. The Final Declaration stated that consultations about elections should be held between representatives of the two zones from 29 July 1955 onwards. Four days before that date Diem rejected any proposal from the Vietminh unless they could prove that they would 'put the superior interests of the national community above those of Communism'.[15] Instead of dicussing elections, the authorities in South Vietnam encouraged demonstrations against communist 'misdeeds' and against the Geneva agreement. In Saigon the police arrested more than 100 men and women for demonstrating in favour of consultations about elections. Elsewhere in the south people were imprisoned for explaining the provisions of the settlement to their friends.[16]

The Vietminh, on the other hand, reaffirmed the agreements, pointing out that the division of the country was intended to be temporary and demanding that elections be arranged. They warned the south on 6 June 1955 that whoever tried to partition Vietnam was the enemy of the Vietnamese people and would surely be defeated.[17] However they had no hope against the Americans who were determined to maintain a non-communist regime in the south. The NSC policy statement of August 1954 had made clear the lengths to which they were prepared to go. Not only would the president use his executive power to authorize overt and covert support; he would also, if necessary, get Congressional authority to use military forces locally or against any outside pressures, including Communist China. Such action would be taken to defeat 'local Communist subversion or rebellion *not constituting armed attack*'.[18] [italics added] Thus the US leaders were ready to seize upon any move made by the Vietminh as a pretext for intervening in Vietnam.

Lacking any countervailing support from China or the Soviet Union, the Vietminh could only look on while Diem perpetuated the partition of Vietnam. Not only did he block elections: he also sealed the border between the two halves of the country. After rejecting a North Vietnamese request for the opening of trade relations he also prevented any postal exchange between the two regions, thus keeping totally apart thousands of families whose members had been divided by the vagaries of war.[19] Regardless of the desire of most Vietnamese for a united country Diem consolidated his own power. In October 1955 he arranged a referendum to determine the form of government in the south. Ostensibly there was a choice between a monarchy under the playboy Bao Dai and a republic led by Diem. In practice the result was foregone. Diem received what even American observers described as a 'too resounding' 98.2 per cent of the vote.[20] Although somewhat embarrassed by such blatant gerrymandering, the US government was pleased with its protege. Aid poured in: by 1956 it totalled $250 million per annum, most of it earmarked for 'security'. The Pentagon history cites the example of a twenty-mile highway, built at the request of the US Military Assistance Advisory Group, which was allocated more money than the total sum provided for labour, community development, social welfare, health and education between 1954 and 1961.[21]

Such an order of priorities did no harm to Diem's reputation among the Americans. During the first years of his rule he was hailed as a hero in the USA – the 'tough miracle man' who, having halted 'the red tide of Communism in Asia', was creating a new nation in South Vietnam. In 1961 Vice-President Johnson described him as 'the Winston Churchill of Asia'. Also in 1961 a State Department paper claimed that between 1956 and 1960 there had been 'something close to an economic miracle in South Vietnam'. The production of foodstuffs, textiles and other consumer goods had risen dramatically. Diem's government, it claimed, had successfully settled 900,000 refugees from the north; had helped 300,000 tenant farmers with an agrarian reform programme and had increased loans to peasant families five-fold between 1957 and 1959. A rural health scheme had provided dispensaries for half the villages and hamlets. Between 1956 and 1960 the elementary school population had risen from 400,000 to 1,500,000. The State Department concluded that it was 'a record of progress over a few brief years equalled by few young countries'.[22]

Despite the fulsome public acclaim for Diem, some Americans had considerable private reservations about his government. An intelligence report of May 1959 noted that a façade of representative institutions concealed an essentially authoritarian regime. Intelligence experts also cast doubt on Diem's agrarian reforms. Far from redistributing land to the poor peasants, the government had returned to the landlords those holdings that had been given to the peasants by the Vietminh. Thus 15 per cent of the people

still owned 75 per cent of the land. Furthermore, a report com-
piled at the beginning of 1960 by the US Embassy in Saigon
claimed that Diem's coercive measures had made the population
apathetic and resentful; there was no rapport between the
government and the people.[23]

American criticisms at this stage were largely confined to
confidential documents and reports. Even in 1961, however, some
doubts were expressed openly about the economic miracle. In an
article sub-titled 'Lavish aid limited progress', an American
economist argued that South Vietnam was excessively reliant on
the large US aid programme which had been directed to military
spending and importing consumer goods. Instead of stimulating
economic growth it had encouraged the Saigon regime to be a
permanent mendicant. The withdrawal of aid would leave the
army unpaid and the civilian population unfed. In the light of
those facts, the economist's verdict was that the US government
had built a 'castle in sand'.[24]

That judgment assumed, of course, that the aim of the aid
programme was to encourage the South Vietnamese to create a
viable economy. If, however, its prime purpose was to benefit the
US economy it might be considered highly successful. According
to one view, the aid programme enabled US corporations to
establish bridgeheads from which they assumed complete control
over the economy of South Vietnam.[25]

Whatever its true objective the programme in fact left the mass of
the Vietnamese as poor as they were before it began. While 90
per cent of the population were peasants only 3 per cent of American
aid went on rural projects.[26] Disgruntled peasants swelled the
mounting criticism of the regime. Despite repression, the non-
communist opposition was becoming, by 1960, increasingly
vehement. At the beginning of November an influential journal
warned that the people were being badgered into a revolution.
Since the most elementary rights were denied, it was necessary to
replace the government by forceful means. The right-of-centre
nationalists felt that they must act quickly: there was a race
against the clock between the Vietminh and themselves.[27]

Diem's dictatorship was creating the very revolution that for
years he had worked to prevent. In 1955 he initiated an 'anti-
communist' denunciation campaign which resulted in the deten-
tion of between 50,000 and 100,000 people. The camps held not

only communists but also the leaders of religious sects and the smaller political parties, together with journalists and trade-unionists who were 'unco-operative'.[28] The rounding up of opponents became more frequent and brutal during 1958 when the methods of the security forces antagonized many villagers. 'A certain sequence of events became almost classical: denunciation, encirclement of villages, searches and raids, arrests of suspects, plunderings, interrogations enlivened sometimes by torture (even of innocent people), deportation, and "regrouping" of populations suspected of intelligence with the rebels . . .'[29] The Self-Defence Corps and the Civil Guard who carried out such operations were usually ill-trained, poorly equipped and badly led. Their brutality and misconduct turned many peasants into revolutionaries.[30]

Persecuted nationalists and harassed peasants were outside critics. There was also growing disillusion about Diem within the ranks of the government itself. One of its causes was the outrageous nepotism practised by the Ngo family.

Diem's brother, Ngo Dinh Nhu, was his political adviser, with an authority rivalling that of the president himself. The Can Lao Party, created by Nhu in 1954 and responsible to him, wielded immense power, partly because all government officials assumed that it was very powerful. Nhu was also the author of the regime's official philosophy, Personalism – 'an incomprehensible hodge-podge having something to do with state power, the dignity of the Person . . . and the virtues of humility, renunciation and sacrifice.'[31] Such virtues were conspicuously lacking in Nhu's wife, known to US journalists as 'the Dragon Lady'. She was a powerful person in her own right: the First Lady of South Vietnam (Diem being a bachelor), a member of the National Assembly and a leading figure in the Women's Solidarity League, a para-military organization for the defence of the ruling clique. (Her father was Ambassador in Washington.) In family discussions she spurred on her husband and brothers-in-law to impose the authoritarian rule she felt the country required.

Ngo Dinh Can, another brother of the president, needed no prompting. Throughout the period of the regime he was dictator of the whole of central Vietnam. Another important member of the family was Archbishop Ngo Dinh Thuc, the eldest brother and one of Diem's closest advisers. The youngest brother, Ngo Dinh Luyen, who had little influence, served as Ambassador to Britain.

The Ngo family was adept at turning its power to its own material advantage: corruption and nepotism went hand in hand. Nhu financed himself and his various subversive organizations by means of extortion, illicit opium trading and currency swindles. Ngo Dinh Can treated central Vietnam as a personal business enterprise, controlling the local shipping and cinnamon trade and keeping officials under his thumb by graft and extortion. Madame Nhu also acquired a personal fortune in goods which could easily be converted into assets in Europe. She was said to have owned, *inter alia*, a large theatre on the Champs Elysées.[32] Ngo Dinh Diem, himself concerned with power rather than feathering his own nest, turned a blind eye on the depredations of his rapacious relations.

The historical significance of such corruption was that, for the Ngo family, the maintenance of its own power and prestige took precedence over all else. The fate of South Vietnam was, by comparison, of secondary importance. Diem trusted no one outside his family and adopted a policy of 'divide and rule' to prevent strangers usurping his authority. So determined was he to ensure that no rivals could emerge, that he even sabotaged military operations and replaced officers who were competent with those who were corruptible. He was, as someone suggested, not so much running a government as running an opposition within it.[33]

On 11 November 1960 a number of army officers, led by Colonel Nguyen Chahn Thi, attempted a *coup d'état* in which paratroops besieged the presidential palace and occupied a number of key points in Saigon. The rebels promised to establish 'true democracy and liberty' in South Vietnam and to continue the fight against communism. Freedom of the press, assembly and opinion were to be proclaimed. Within 48 hours the revolt was over. The regime was saved by Diem's divide and rule tactics: in the atmosphere they created the army officers did not trust each other. They feared that the leader of a successful coup might oust the rest of them as well as the Ngos. Thus on 12 November loyal units came to the rescue of Diem who declared that the rebels had been thwarted by the 'hand of God'.[34]

With the failure of that right-wing nationalist plot, the initiative passed to Diem's enemies on the left, who provided convenient scapegoats for Diem and his allies in the United States. American officials denied that there were any legitimate grounds for dissatisfaction with the government. They attributed the trouble to a communist campaign of armed action, subversion and terror, instigated and directed by North Vietnam. According to their theory South Vietnam had outstripped the North, particularly in economic growth. Unable to accept that situation, the leaders in Hanoi had 'decided on a course of violence'.[35] In order to see that allegation in perspective we turn now to the developments in North Vietnam in the years following the Geneva Conference.

Four

THE DEVELOPMENT OF THE NORTH: RESISTANCE TO DIEM

Ho Chi Minh, having 'snatched compromise out of the jaws of victory',[1] was faced with a major problem when he returned to Hanoi in October 1954. While he hoped shortly to gain control of the whole of Vietnam, he had in the meanwhile to create a viable political and economic entity in only half a country. That half had, moreover, suffered most in the recent fighting. Even before it was devastated by the conflict between the French and the Vietminh it had been plundered by the Japanese and then in 1946 by the Chinese Nationalists. During the Second World War its roads and railways had been bombed by the US Air Force. Perhaps most serious of all, the area north of the seventeenth parallel was cut off from the main source of its staple diet, rice, which lay in the Mekong Delta. A contemporary French authority on Vietnam, stressing the economic importance of the south, with its large rice surplus and its exports of rubber, pepper, coffee and precious woods, predicted that Ho's regime, deprived of those benefits, would face either starvation or a dependence on Communist China which would be tantamount to annexation.[2]

One of Ho Chi Minh's first priorities was, therefore, the development of agriculture. In the first year of the new government famine was avoided only by a Russian-financed purchase of rice from Burma. The government believed that greater production would be encouraged by a re-allocation of the land. It thus continued a land reform campaign which had begun in the areas controlled by the Vietminh during the war. From 1954 to 1956 the countryside was thrown into chaos as a result of an eruption of violence and terror. The reform was carried out by inexperienced cadres who received little training before being turned loose in the villages. In the villages many people seized the chance to settle old scores.

It has been commonly accepted that thousands of innocent

people were killed and imprisoned; that the brutality of the cadres resulted in a veritable bloodbath. More recently, however, it has been claimed that the source on which much of the discussion of the land reform is based is extremely dubious. According to one view it consists largely of fabrications and serious mistranslations. That view has received support from an unlikely source. In 1972 Nguyen Van Chau, director of the Psychological War Service of the South Vietnamese Armed Forces from 1956 to 1962, stated that the alleged 'Communist bloodbath' was '100 percent fabricated' by US-financed Saigon intelligence services.[3]

Whether or not the slaughter was as terrible as some have alleged, it does appear that the programme got seriously out of hand. The government itself admitted that 'mistakes' had been made and promised corrections. At the end of October 1956 Truong Chinh, the head of the campaign, was replaced as Secretary-General of the Lao Dong Party by Ho Chi Minh. The minister of agriculture was also dismissed. During November the government announced the release of 12,000 people from prison and labour camps. The People's Agricultural Reform Tribunals, which allegedly sentenced many innocent people to death and imprisonment, were abolished. A programme of 'democratization' promised greater freedom of movement, improved living conditions, increased powers for the National Assembly and the holding of elections in 1957.[4] Fitzgerald has argued that the rectification campaign was a remarkable achievement: that it was perhaps the only occasion when a communist leader has admitted that he and his party were in error on a major issue. Taking into account the communist attitude to politics, she points out that the equivalent in the West would be for a leader to confess to treason.[5]

Thanks to the government's change of policy the disaffection gradually subsided. There was of course no return to the old system: the power of the landlords was destroyed. Subsequently it was claimed that the removal of the landlords 'lifted a yoke' from the peasants and released their considerable energies, which the government channelled into agricultural co-operatives.[6] At the end of 1960 there were more than 40,000 co-operatives which included more than 85 per cent of all farming families.[7] After a disastrous beginning the agrarian policy achieved some success. The yield per hectare of raw rice increased. Better

6. North Vietnamese peasants on a collective farm near Haiphong.

hydraulic works and irrigation systems gave more crops per year in each field. Consequently a growth rate of about 3 per cent per annum (a considerable achievement for a developing country) was achieved in the early 1960s. Increasing population meant that the problem of providing enough food remained acute. Starvation, an old scourge of the Vietnamese peasant, was, however, eliminated and a five-year plan for 1961–5 promised further improvement.

The government of North Vietnam intended to have a balanced economy. While they aimed at increasing agricultural production they also pressed ahead with the reconstruction and expansion of industry. Their legacy from the French was not particularly impressive. There were two major industrial enterprises, the cement works at Haiphong and textile plants at Haiphong and Nam Dinh. In addition they had a useful railway system, port installations, a few electric power plants and some other minor factories. Everything was, after a devastating war, in a very poor state of repair. It was fortunate for Ho that considerable foreign aid was made available from the Soviet bloc and China. Between 1955 and 1961 grants and loans totalled more than $1,000,000,000. As a result of the aid and their own efforts the North Vietnamese made significant industrial progress. Buttinger, an American historian, who was for some years a strong supporter of Diem, has commented that, while the masses had to accept austerity, North Vietnam, even before 1960, was 'well on the road toward becoming the most industrialized country of Southeast Asia'. Ho's regime, he noted, had built modern factories and had trained its owned skilled personnel. Less than ten years after its industrialization began it was producing items which were still not being produced in the south: machine tools, electric motors, office equipment, bicycle tyres and even small ocean craft.[8]

In the light of North Vietnam's achievements in industry and agriculture, it is hard to accept the official American view that the communist leaders decided to resort to force in 1959 because they could not take over South Vietnam in any other way and because the south was socially and economically 'far outstripping the North'. That interpretation becomes even more difficult to uphold against the background of other policies pursued by the North Vietnamese.

As already noted, the North Vietnamese government pressed hard for the elections in 1956, only to be ignored by Diem. It continued to urge negotiations on the basis of free general elections by secret ballot in July 1957, March 1958 and as late as July 1959 and 1960. Diem either rebuffed or ignored each initiative, confident that the US would underwrite him. While he knew that the Americans were ready to intervene militarily, his opponents were aware that the help they could expect from their Soviet and Chinese friends would probably be 'restricted to kind words, warm gestures of solidarity, and propaganda campaigns'.[9] The Chinese communists had consistently argued that revolution could not be exported, that the success of revolutionary movements depended on the efforts of the indigenous people. In any case, surrounded as they were by US bases, they were scarcely able to exert much pressure on an ally of America. The Soviet leaders during this period were promoting a policy of peaceful co-existence with the West, and in particular with the United States. Thus they were anxious to reduce tension, not to increase it by impinging on an area where the Americans were, even at this stage, well-entrenched. Furthermore, during the late 1950s a split gradually emerged between China and the Soviet Union. By 1960 it was already pronounced, as was the unlikelihood of any co-ordinated action by both powers on behalf of the North Vietnamese. While both were ready to give aid to the North, they gave little encouragement to a more aggressive policy against Diem.

For some time the consensus, even among the Northern leadership, was opposed to any major move against the government in the south. Ho and his colleagues were, of course, keen to see Vietnam unified under themselves. After 1956, however, they felt that their victory would come later rather than sooner. In January 1957 the National Assembly recognized that 'the struggle for unity would be long and difficult'.[10] An essential first step would be to consolidate the revolution in the north. (Their Soviet allies evidently shared their expectation of a lengthy struggle. At the beginning of 1957 at the United Nations the USSR proposed the simultaneous admission of both Vietnams!) At the end of 1956 the Saigon regime was indeed confident enough to talk of liberating the north where it considered 'the fall of the illegitimate regime was near'.[11]

While the North Vietnamese limited themselves to verbal protests, Diem did not hesitate to use force against the communists. We have already noted some of the consequences of his repression. In the long run it was counter-productive since it provoked a rebellion against him. For a time, however, he seemed fully in control. Major campaigns against the communists in 1956 and 1957 weakened the remnants of the Vietminh in the south. One cadre who survived explained that the official line of the Southern Vietminh from 1954 to 1959 was to carry on a legal, political, non-violent form of struggle. Towards the end of 1959 it allowed 'violence for self-defence'. The first policy – of non-violence – cost the lives of many of his comrades. Nevertheless, despite Diem and the 'strictly legal' line many former Vietminh members were still available for action when the call came.[12]

It appears that during 1959 communist leaders in North and

South Vietnam realized that the time had come to take up arms against Diem: if they were not prepared to give a lead there would be spontaneous uprisings against his rule. In May 1959 the Central Committee of the Lao Dong party voted in favour of fighting 'jointly and severally' for the liberation of Vietnam.[13] Having advised patience and non-violent opposition for several years they were beginning to change their line. They could hardly be accused of being precipitate.

In March 1960 the South Vietnamese 'Veterans of the Resistance association' declared that they were fighting to end the 'Fascist dictatorship of the Ngo family' and to set up 'a democratic government of national union in South Vietnam'. They anticipated that such a government would discuss with North Vietnam how to achieve the peaceful re-unification of the Fatherland.[14] An official from North Vietnam who attended the meeting, reported to Hanoi the strength of popular pressures, warning of a forthcoming struggle which would involve the north. The issue of re-unification and the question of what support should be given to the south were discussed at the Third Congress of the Lao Dong party in September 1960. There it was agreed that more should be done to liberate the South Vietnamese people from imperialism. In addition, Ho Chi Minh gave up the secretaryship of the party in favour of Le Duan who before 1954 had been chief political commissar for the southern guerrillas, thus assuring even closer liaison with the south.[15]

Despite such moves, the congress was not primarily a sabre-rattling occasion. The main Soviet delegate emphasized that peaceful co-existence was the only line completely in accord with the ultimate aim of communism. According to a communiqué issued after Soviet–Vietnamese talks which followed the congress, there was complete identity of views on both sides.[16] Such was also the opinion of a staunchly anti-communist commentator who felt the congress had indicated that North Vietnam would follow the Russian policy of peaceful co-existence based on the possibility of avoiding war. It had indeed announced a major defence cut to provide money for economic development.[17]

Our examination of the policies of Ho Chi Minh's government between 1954 and 1960 suggests that they were concerned rather to develop a socialist system in the north than to subvert the regime of Diem in the south. (Although they obviously disliked that regime.) The Saigon–Washington claim that the fighting in South Vietnam, which led to the second Indochina war, was the result of aggression by Hanoi, is not borne out by the evidence. (There is some evidence, indeed that the South was guilty of deploying small saboteur groups against the North.)[18] The outbreak of fighting was in the main provoked by Diem's regime. Naturally the communists did not hesitate to take advantage of his errors and eventually played a major role in the opposition which emerged. To understand the nature of the conflict which followed we must consider what kind of opposition it was.

As already noted, in 1954 the People's Army of Vietnam was regrouped north of the seventeenth parallel. While the regular troops were withdrawn, many other members of the Vietminh remained in the south. Like the organization as a whole, the southern Vietminh were not all communists. There was, however, a hard core of communist cadres who became the leaders of a new resistance movement. By 1958 they had established cells in former Vietminh strongholds: in the U Minh forest at the southern tip of the Mekong Delta, in the jungles to the west of Saigon, in the jungle area of the northern province Quang Nam and elsewhere.[19] Gradually they gained support, moving from their base areas to neighbouring villages where they gathered-in a variety of recruits.

There were those who were quite simply hostile to any government. In many other villages there were branches of the religious sects whom Diem had suppressed. The cadres assiduously fanned their hatred. They also exploited the fact that Diem came from Hué in central Vietnam and that many of his officials were refugees from the north. Southerners themselves, they turned regional animosity to their advantage, keeping in the background the eventual aim of re-unification with their northern comrades. Their best recruiting sergeant was Diem himself. As a result of his brutality, 'the people were like a mound of straw, ready to be ignited'.[20] Included in the combustible material were montagnard tribesmen, forced to leave their traditional homelands to be re-settled in more 'secure' areas, and the many peasants who had been removed from their ancestral villages and forced to live in agrovilles.[21]

Between 1958 and 1960 the cadres were occupied moulding their recruits into resistance groups rather than actively resisting. Before 1959 spontaneous acts of terrorism, including numerous assassinations had been carried out against the official line: towards the end of that year the groups were fully activated. In late September two government battalions were ambushed by guerrillas in the Plain of Reeds, southwest of Saigon. After a brief fight twelve government troops were killed and the rest surrendered. According to Halberstam, it was from this time that the guerrillas became known as the Vietcong.[22] The term 'Vietcong' means 'Vietnamese Communist' and was coined by the Saigon regime as a derogatory description which implied that anyone who fought against Diem was a communist. That implication was unjustified: the opposition was in fact much more widely based.

In December 1960 various oppositionist groups (including communists and non-communists) coalesced to form a National Front for the Liberation of South Vietnam (Mat-Tran dan-Toc giaiphong), commonly known as the National Liberation Front. Somewhere in South Vietnam, perhaps in Tay Ninh province, a hundred delegates representing a dozen or more political parties and religious groups formed a broad coalition, which has been described as 'the Vietminh reborn'.[23] Its objectives, specified in a ten-point programme, were nationalist rather than Marxist. Just as the Vietminh had emphasized opposition to French colonialism, so the NLF called for the overthrow of 'the camouflaged colonial regime' established by the USA. Disregarding the tensions that existed between Diem and the Americans, the Front attacked the 'servile', Yankee-dominated regime in the south. Their aim was to replace Diem with a government, representing all social classes, nationalities and religions, to be formed from the anti-Diemist parties. The new government would ensure essential democratic liberties, including the right of all patriotic organizations, whatever their politics, to carry on normal activities. It would also improve living conditions and implement land reform.

The new government was to pursue a neutralist foreign policy. Diplomatic relations would be established with all countries, regardless of their political complexion. Furthermore, South Vietnam was to remain outside all power blocs and to refuse any military alliance. The most crucial issue of foreign policy was the relationship with North Vietnam. Point IX of the Front's programme advocated the peaceful re-unification of both zones by stages 'on the basis of negotiations and through the seeking of ways and means in conformity with the interests of the Vietnamese nation'.[24]

Political programmes are notoriously unreliable as predictors of actual as opposed to proposed policy. Any programme in which there was communist participation was doubly suspect. Thus the NLF programme, and indeed the whole movement, was simply dismissed by Diem and his US allies as a convenient cover for Hanoi. They failed to perceive that the emergence of the Front marked not a mass shift to Marxism but a crisis of confidence within South Vietnam. The nature of that crisis becomes clearer if we focus our attention on the villages.

We have seen that the North Vietnamese put land reform at the top of their agenda. It appeared to be a bloody business until the government intervened at the end of 1956 to 'correct' some of the 'errors'.[25] Nevertheless it did finally end the rule of the landlords, which was the necessary first step to improving the lot of the peasants. Wherever landlordism survives so also does peasant discontent. Under Diem the landlords did not merely survive but positively thrived. They first delayed then emasculated land reform in South Vietnam. Nothing at all was attempted in 1954; in 1955 a few tentative moves were made to safeguard tenants' rights. Not until 1956 was there any significant distribution of land. Even then the programme was balked and five years after it began over a million tenants had received no land at all. Many other peasants were aggrieved at having to pay for land they considered their own. Under the Vietminh, large landowners had been dispossessed. Under Diem, peasants who had been given their land were obliged to pay for it at rates they could not afford. Buttinger has pointed out that, while Diem had the power to eradicate landlordism, he was too conservative to do so. Such a drastic social change was repugnant to him; instead he helped the landlords to keep the peasants in subjection.[26]

As opposition in the countryside grew, Diem appointed his own officials to maintain contact with and control over the villages. They personified the government's intrusion into the lives of its citizens – an intrusion alien to Vietnamese tradition. For centuries the villages, under the direction of their own notables, had met the demands of the central authority without undue external supervision and from a sense of obligation to the emperor. The villagers felt no such obligation to Diem who simply coerced them into obedience.

The consequence of his heavy-handed conservatism was a widening gap in the countryside between the rulers and the ruled. The status and influence of those who had given the villages some sense of community had been eroded. Instead, the regime attempted to impose cohesion by force, thus inviting the formation of a counter-élite to occupy the vacuum it had created. The communist cadres and other NLF leaders did what Diem's officials neglected to do. They listened to the grievances of the peasants and, having gained their confidence, persuaded many of them that the remedy was to build a new kind of society. During a period of discord and dissension they offered a new consensus. What made Diem's regime particularly vulnerable to their approach was not merely the reaction to its use of terror but also the fact that, in so many ways, it was simply failing in its duty as a government. Unlike the old traditional system on the one hand and the NLF at the other end of the political spectrum, Diem's clique failed to establish any rapport with the Vietnamese people.

Having forged its links with the people, the NLF was able to organize an increasingly effective opposition. While Diem managed to crush the revolt of his own troops in November 1960, he could not prevent the countryside going over to his enemies. By mid-1961 US intelligence services reported that NLF membership had reached 15,000, half of whom were fully armed.[27] Shortly after he took office President Kennedy learned from his experts that large areas of the countryside in South Vietnam were 'under considerable Communist control' and that the Vietcong were encircling Saigon itself. There was a widespread feeling that Diem was unable to rally his people against the communists because of his 'reliance on virtual one-man rule, his toleration of corruption . . . and his refusal to relax a rigid system of public controls'.[28] How to achieve American goals in Vietnam with such an unpromising ally was a major problem for the new President.

Five

KENNEDY AND THE GROWING AMERICAN INVOLVEMENT

President Kennedy accepted the objectives in Vietnam laid down by his predecessors. He reiterated the claim that the United States' main purpose was to preserve South Vietnam's independence. In his first State of the Union message he reminded his fellow-citizens of the threat of international communism: '. . . in Asia, the relentless pressures of the Chinese Communists menace the security of the entire area – from the borders of India and South Viet Nam to the jungles of Laos . . .'[1] Thus, he argued, the US commitment to 'Free Vietnam' was intended not only to preserve the independence of the South Vietnamese but also to maintain America's prestige and influence as the chief bastion of the whole 'Free World'. In the latter part of his presidency Kennedy expressed in private some reservations about the US role in Asia. All his public statements, however, emphasized the importance of taking a stand in Vietnam.

During his first months in office he was even more forceful in private than in his public pronouncements. On 11 May 1961 he ordered the deployment of 400 'Special Forces' in South Vietnam, together with 100 other US advisers. Those moves were not disclosed to the public, nor was his decision to begin a secret war against North Vietnam. Intelligence agents were covertly infiltrated into the North, sabotage teams established and leaflets dropped by air incited the people to rise against their leaders. Teams were also sent to Southeast Laos to attack Vietcong bases and lines of communication. In addition, American advisers trained the South Vietnamese army to carry out 'ranger' raids against the North.[2] At the beginning of the Kennedy administration Khrushchev, the Soviet leader, had made a major speech in favour of wars of national liberation which was interpreted, probably mistakenly, as a challenge to the United States. Suddenly, one observer noted, 'the stopping of guerrilla warfare became a great fad.' Kennedy

7. **An American adviser on patrol with South Vietnamese troops.**

himself became fascinated with unconventional warfare and considered that counter-guerrilla and counter-revolutionary training would pay handsome dividends. The Vietcong would, he thought, be beaten at their own game, and at quite a modest cost.[3]

He failed to understand that what made the guerrillas a formidable force was the support they drew from the people. Their capacity to convince the peasants that they were both fighting the same fight was their great strength. Their skill at living in the jungle and in mounting ambushes was important but secondary. Such skills might be acquired at the Special Warfare School at Fort Bragg; there was, however, no course which could teach the GIs to win the trust of Vietnamese peasants.

Experiments with special forces were in the main ineffectual and were not enough to satisfy the US military establishment. Throughout the summer and autumn of 1961 Kennedy was under pressure to send American ground combat troops against the Vietcong. The situation was undoubtedly serious, as General Maxwell Taylor, the President's special military adviser, reported after a fact-finding mission to South Vietnam. Taylor recommended sending US troops to raise national morale in the South and to show other countries in Southeast Asia that America was determined to resist a communist takeover. He believed that Americans could give the South Vietnamese army 'the élan and style needed to win'. A price would be paid for those benefits: the presence of US combat troops would increase international tension and accentuate the risk of a major war in Asia.[4] While Kennedy's generals were sure the price was worth paying, he had some doubts. He appreciated that having given way once, he would soon be asked to send even more men. 'It's like taking a drink,' he said. 'The effect wears off, and you have to take another.'[5]

Nevertheless, he did give in partially to the demands of the military. In November 1961 he agreed to send more support troops and advisers, while still demurring at the use of combat units. At the end of 1960 US forces in Vietnam numbered 773; by the end of 1963 there were 16,500. Inevitably the advisers and support troops were involved in actual combat. The numbers of Americans killed and wounded rose from 14 in 1961 to 109 in 1962 and then to 489 in 1963. In addition to more men Kennedy also provided more materials of war, including helicopters and other aircraft.[6]

Superficially there appeared to be little change in US policy – rather more of the same mixture. The theory was still that the South Vietnamese should be helped to help themselves, without involving too deeply the United States. Once again, as in 1954 under Eisenhower, the administration tried to ensure that their money was being well spent. The increased help was made conditional on concrete demonstrations by Diem that he was 'prepared to work in an orderly way . . . and broaden the political base of the regime'. Kennedy's actions seemed to be minor variations on a well-worn theme.[7]

Retrospectively, however, it has been claimed that Kennedy transformed the 'limited-risk gamble' of the Eisenhower years into a 'broad commitment' to prevent the communist domination of South Vietnam.[8] There is some truth in that judgment. In refusing to send combat troops, Kennedy felt that he had acted moderately and that he was therefore justified in being aggressive in his speeches, thus satisfying different shades of opinion in the

USA. In his public statements on Vietnam he 'markedly escalated the rhetoric and the rationale for being there'.[9] They had the effect of moving the Vietnam war nearer the forefront of American politics and of encouraging the generals, who were adept at seizing their chances, to seek a greater share in the shaping of policy. Their pressure had already helped to increase US spending considerably and had put many more men into the battle zones. During 1962 they pressed their demands at a number of points.

8. **An American helicopter bringing in supplies to a South Vietnamese village.**

They requested new jet planes for use in Vietnam; on this issue the President did not accommodate them. They also wanted free-fire zones (initially areas where unused bombs could be jettisoned), unrestricted use of napalm and widespread defoliation of the enemy's jungle refuges. Kennedy was doubtful about those demands; in particular he was appalled by the use of napalm against living targets. Nevertheless, the generals succeeded in winning his consent for a restricted use of napalm (who could

monitor that restriction?), for defoliation against lines of communication and for limited free-fire zones.[10] We can see here the
early stages of the process whereby the US military began effectively
to determine policy in Vietnam. Despite his reservations, Kennedy
found it increasingly difficult to resist his generals once he had
opened the door to them.

The long-term effects of his policy were to be felt during
President Johnson's administration. One of the short-term results
was the tightening of the bonds that linked the US government
with the Diem regime. Attempts to impose conditions on the help
he received were futile while he was the only viable anti-
communist leader in the South. As one American journalist
succinctly commented, the United States was bound to 'sink or
swim with Ngo Dinh Diem'.[11] Continuing to support Diem
and also allowing more initiative to US military leaders were
policies which complemented each other. Under Diem there was
no prospect of political reform. Thus there could be only a military
response to a worsening situation. Kennedy's zeal for counter-
insurgency and fashionable discussion about winning over the
'hearts and minds' of the Vietnamese people created the illusion
that his administration saw the problem as essentially political.
The fact is that only lip-service was paid to the importance of the
political situation, as was demonstrated by the Strategic Hamlets
Programme.

The objectives of that programme were to cut off the guerrillas
from the peasants on whose support they relied and, at the same
time, give the peasants the 'security' to allow them to choose
'freely' between the South Vietnamese government and the
Vietcong. It resembled the 'agroville' scheme, started in 1959,
whereby Diem planned to resettle about three hundred thousand
peasants over a period of some four years. The agrovilles were
fortified reserves where the peasants would no longer be
accessible to the guerrillas. They drew their inspiration from the
successful resettlement of the Chinese 'squatters' by the British
during the Malayan emergency. As we have seen, the situation in
Vietnam was very different from Malaya.[12] Whereas the British
had to cope with a comparatively small-scale resettlement, the
Diem regime, with its customary ineptitude, started a much more
ambitious scheme. Almost without exception, the agrovilles failed
in their objective. Apart from the gross corruption and inefficiency

of its champions, the whole scheme was under-financed and had not taken into account the depth of peasant resentment. Its consequences were greater discontent in the countryside and a boost to the resistance movement.

Despite that fiasco, a new resettlement programme, based on the notion of strategic hamlets, was devised – according to Bernard Fall, 'the most mammoth example of "social engineering" in the non-Communist world'.[13] Launched in the Mekong Delta early in 1962, by August it extended throughout the whole country. At the end of September the regime claimed that over one-third of the total rural population had been resettled. There were indeed many so-called strategic hamlets. Provincial officials, terrified of offending Nhu (who posed as the scheme's originator) and anxious to receive US aid earmarked for the programme, competed to build as many as possible. One American wryly commented that if you stood still long enough they would 'throw a piece of barbed wire around you and call you a strategic hamlet'.[14] Quantitatively they may have seemed impressive: in every other respect they were, like the agrovilles, a total failure.

The villagers were almost always resettled forcibly, sometimes being pushed at gunpoint into the 'security' of the hamlets. Areas surrounding the hamlets were declared 'open zones' where aerial and artillery bombardment served as an extra inducement to move into the hamlet and stay there. While the scheme helped to line the pockets of the provincial chiefs and gave Diem the illusion of controlling his own people, the people themselves suffered great hardship. For them, the programme entailed, in the words of a US Marine Colonel, 'forced resettlement, physical oppression, coercion, and political "persuasion" by the club'.[15] The first of those was the worst. Vietnamese peasants worshipped their ancestors and expressed their reverence by tending ancestral graves. The land where they lay was sacred and formed part of the peasants' social identity. When they were driven from that land the links with their ancestors were snapped. They felt totally lost in a strange world, although geographically it may not have been very distant from their own village. Their feeling of disorientation often produced results diametrically opposed to those intended. Fitzgerald has pointed out that forced resettlement might drive a peasant 'off the edges of his old life', thus exposing him directly to 'the political movement that could best provide him with a new

9. **A North Vietnamese anti-aircraft unit.**

identity'.[16] Even those who did not join the guerrillas were, by the very act of relocation, turned against the government.

Many did join the Vietcong. Ironically, one of the alleged aims of the Strategic Hamlets Programme had been to allow the peasants a 'free choice' between the government and its opponents. An American official later commented that one of the reasons for its failure was that Vietcong supporters and agents had managed to remain in the hamlets and continue their subversion. Clearly that was disastrous: there could be no 'free choice' between the government and the communists while the Vietcong were allowed to exist![17]

They were not merely existing: their numbers were increasing. An American intelligence memorandum at the end of 1962 – when one third of South Vietnam's peasants were supposedly safely ensconced in strategic hamlets – stated that the Vietcong had 'expanded the size and enhanced the capability and organization of its guerrilla force'.[18] Since January its élite troops had grown from some 16,500 to about 23,000, supported by some 100,000 irregulars. Although the government mustered about 285,000 men, including regulars and para-military groups, they could not prevent the Vietcong controlling about one-fifth of the villages and infiltrating the urban areas. As one observer remarked, the circle of artillery and barbed wire around the strategic hamlets 'enclosed a political void that waited for the NLF'.[19] By the beginning of 1963, according to official US figures, about half the population of South Vietnam supported the National Liberation Front. Such statistics were tucked away in confidential reports. In public all was said to be going well – the strategic hamlets were undermining the VC and the guerrilla war was being won by the government forces. Those dangerous illusions were fostered by, among others, a man who might have been expected to sound the alarm.

General Paul D. Harkins was appointed head of the US Military Advisory Command (MACV) in January 1962. On his arrival at Saigon he told reporters that he was an optimist and that he intended to have optimists on his staff.[20] Under his direction, information was processed to provide the success stories that would please his superiors in Washington. Officers filing pessimistic reports were sacked and their statements suppressed. Critical journalists were upbraided and told to 'get on the team'. Under Diem the war was being lost. Instead of trying to correct the faults, the US Embassy in Saigon and MACV joined with Diem's officials in pretending that the VC were at the end of their tether. Harkins was a man of 'compelling mediocrity' who was carrying out what he conceived as his orders. His talented superiors were even more at fault.

Maxwell Taylor, Chairman of the Joint Chiefs of Staff from 1962 to 1964, consistently supported his old friend Harkins. Having been responsible for appointing Harkins to MACV, he was perhaps unwilling to admit his own mistake. Robert McNamara, the Secretary of Defense, who later was to comment that Harkins 'wasn't worth a damn', proved to be as gullible as Taylor. A great expert in evaluating data, McNamara simply accepted all the distorted statistics from Saigon and naturally got the wrong answer. On his numerous visits to Vietnam he failed to see even what was in front of him. His trips, carefully arranged by Harkins to show the bright side, gave McNamara an illusion of knowledge rather than a genuine understanding of the situation.[21]

While Diem and his US allies deluded themselves, partly because they could not afford to face the truth, the people of South Vietnam had no reason to close their eyes to what was happening. They saw that the regime was under increasing strain, with opposition groups beginning to assert themselves in the towns. The government itself was aware of that particular danger and determined to nip protest in the bud. Hence the crisis which eventually brought the downfall of Diem.

It began on 8 May 1963 when government troops in Hué opened fire on militant Buddhists demonstrating against restrictions imposed on their celebration of the anniversary of Buddah's birth. Nine people were killed and several crushed by an armoured car. The government claimed that the deaths and injuries were caused by a grenade thrown into the crowd by an agent of the Vietcong. Even after the true account had been widely circulated it persisted with its lie. Conciliation was not the strong suit of Diem's regime and as the crisis deepened it remained intransigent. Any attempt at compromise would, it felt, be interpreted as weakness.

The Buddhists demanded that the government admit its responsibility for the deaths and pay compensation to the victims' families. When that was refused they began to agitate against the regime. Apart from the issue of compensation they had other reasons for resenting Diem: a Catholic himself he had favoured his co-religionists and discriminated against the Buddhists since 1955. Even religious grievances were only one aspect of the widespread and increasingly vocal hostility to the government. As a Vietnamese academic pointed out during the crisis, the people of Vietnam were no strangers to oppression. They were used to biding their time and when the right time came they found ways of expressing themselves. Since under Diem they did not dare make outright political protests, they gave vent to their feeling through religion.[22] Thanks to Diem's stubbornness and the political acumen of the Buddhist leaders, what might have passed off as a minor incident broadened into a full-scale confrontation.

The most dramatic and harrowing event of the Buddhists' protest was the self-immolation of the monk Thich Quang Duc. On 11 June 1963, seated in the lotus position, he burned himself to death in the centre of Saigon. Halberstam, an eye-witness, recorded: 'Flames were coming from a human being; his body was

10. A Buddhist monk burns himself in protest against the policies of the South Vietnamese government.

slowly withering and shrivelling up, his head blackening and char-
ring . . . As he burned he never moved a muscle, never uttered a
sound, his outward composure in sharp contrast to the wailing
people around him . . . All around this scene of medieval horror
were the signs of modern times: a young Buddhist priest with a
microphone saying calmly over and over again in Vietnamese and
English, "A Buddhist priest burns himself to death. A Buddhist
priest becomes a martyr." '[23] Madame Nhu dismissed the incident
as a 'barbecue' and her husband later commented that if the
Buddhists wished to stage another one he would be 'glad to supply
the gasoline'.[24] In Vietnam and throughout the world millions of
people were horrified by the burning and the callousness of the
Nhus' reaction to it. The American leadership, staggered by the
event and its consequences, attempted to exert pressure on Diem
to make him come to terms with the Buddhists.

There was, however, little chance of reconciliation between
the Buddhists and their growing number of supporters on the one
hand and Diem on the other. Thich Quang Duc had made a remarkable gesture of protest; the response to it prompted his fellow
Buddhists to press home their attack. The regime, in particular the
Nhus, were determined to crush them once for all. While the
Buddhists made the running the government made the mistakes.
Its behaviour was so inept that, in the eyes of one observer, it
appeared to be 'trying to commit suicide'.[25] Perhaps its most
suicidal act was to order raids against Buddhist pagodas by Special
Force troops controlled by Ngo Dinh Nhu.

They launched the attack in a typically underhand way. On
15 August Diem claimed that he had always been in favour of
conciliating the Buddhists. That statement may have been, in part,
a farewell gift for the US ambassador, Nolting, who had since his
appointment in 1961 consistently supported the regime. Guided
by a misplaced sense of duty rather than any reasoned appraisal of
the situation, he had turned a blind eye to all its faults. At the time
of the summer crisis he hoped to refurbish the 'image' of the Ngo
family by urging a reconciliation with the Buddhists. That hope
was soon dashed. Within a week of his departure from Vietnam
he was made to look the fool that he was. On 21 August pagodas
in Saigon, Hué and many other cities were raided and thousands
of monks arrested; some were killed and many of them beaten.
The raids offended not only the Buddhists but also the army,

members of the government itself and also the Americans.[26]

The generals were affronted because Nhu had dressed his special forces as paratroops in order to lay the blame for the raids on the army. Within two days General Le Van Kim was urging the Americans to take a stand against the Nhus to enable the army to displace them.[27] Civilian officials also urged their immediate removal. Diem's defence minister warned the United States not to acquiesce in what they had done; the foreign minister resigned and shaved his head like a Buddhist monk in protest.[28] Many Americans were ready to heed their criticisms. They were appalled by the brutality of the raids and considered the repudiation of Diem's solemn word to Nolting a 'slap in the face for the US'.[29]

For a number of those who directed American policy the pagoda strikes were the last straw. Thereafter they were prepared to disembarrass themselves from Ngo Dinh Nhu and his wife – an action which, given the solidarity of the Ngo family, would precipitate the removal of Diem himself. Henry Cabot Lodge, Nolting's replacement as ambassador, felt it would be disastrous to persist with a totally discredited regime. Less than forty-eight hours after arriving at Saigon he informed the State Department that high ranking Vietnamese generals were sounding out possible American reaction to a coup against Diem. State's reply on 24 August made it clear that the US government could not tolerate a situation in which power continued to lie in Nhu's hands. Diem was to be given a chance to replace Nhu and his coterie. If he refused the US would be forced to consider his own removal and Lodge was instructed to 'urgently examine all possible alternative leadership and make detailed plans as to how we might bring about Diem's replacement if this should become necessary'. State went on to explain that there could be no detailed instructions from Washington about the operation: whatever action Lodge took would be 'backed to the hilt'.[30]

On 29 August Lodge informed Secretary of State Rusk that he agreed with the new line, pointing out that it clearly meant the overthrow of the Diem government. There could be no turning back, he remarked, since US prestige was in large measure already committed to that end and would be even more so as the facts leaked out. Furthermore, said Lodge, there was no possibility that the war could be won under Diem's leadership, nor was there any longer even the slightest prospect that Diem might 'govern the country in a way to gain the support of the people who count . . .'[31] However, despite Lodge's evident apparent eagerness to be rid of the government, the Vietnamese generals made no immediate move.

They could hardly be blamed. For nine years the Americans had backed Diem and when, almost overnight, they changed their tune the generals were nonplussed. Over the years they had learned a healthy respect for Ngo Dinh Nhu and suspected that the latest crisis might be another of his tricks, a manoeuvre to flush out the dissidents in the ranks of the regime. There had always been a close link between Nhu and the US Central Intelligence Agency. How then could the generals trust CIA agents who promised support for a coup to deprive the Ngo family of its power? Fearing betrayal they stood pat. On 31 August Lodge reported to Washington that the conspiracy against Diem had collapsed since the generals had neither the will nor the organization to accomplish anything.[32] To a friend he suggested: 'Perhaps they are like the rest of us, and are afraid to die.'[33] Also on 31 August the National Security Council met in Washington. With the concurrence of Vice-President Johnson and Secretary of Defense McNamara, Rusk insisted that US policy be based on two points: first, they would not pull out of Vietnam until the war was won; secondly, they would not organize a coup against Diem.[34]

The fact was that by the beginning of September US policy regarding Vietnam was in complete disarray, with its leadership divided and in a quandary. Kennedy was as confused as the rest. He was still stuck with Diem while recognizing that he was a hopeless liability. In a television interview on 2 September he suggested that changes in policy and personnel were needed for Diem to regain popular support and improve his chances of winning the war.[35] Various attempts were made to enforce such changes on him. On 14 September the US government announced that it was deferring action on a programme, costing $18.5 million, to finance commercial imports into South Vietnam. Subsequently it suspended such subsidies for trade, imposed a freeze on loans and ceased unconditional financial support for Nhu's special forces.[36]

Although these moves were not announced in public, they were soon well known in Saigon, a city 'keyed-up and alert to every nuance in American policy'. Whatever the precise intentions of the

11. **Saigon civilians huddle behind tanks during the overthrow of Ngo Dinh Diem.**

US leaders, their pressure campaign was bound to encourage those who thought of toppling Diem; the regime itself accused Washington of sabotaging the war effort. During the month of October the generals gradually screwed their courage to the sticking place, convincing themselves that the Americans were indeed serious about supporting a coup. For their part the US leaders were still divided on the issue, although the forces in favour of a coup were becoming stronger. The thinking in Washington was reflected in a message on 30 October from McGeorge Bundy, Kennedy's special assistant for national security, to Lodge. On one hand it warned him to dissuade the generals if he felt that there was not 'clearly a high prospect of success'. However Bundy also stated that 'once a coup under responsible leadership has begun . . . it is in the interest of the US Government that it should succeed'.[37]

In Saigon the time for equivocation had passed. Shortly after 1 p.m. on 1 November the plotters began to take over the city. They seized police headquarters, the radio stations, the airport and attacked the presidential palace and the special forces barracks. Except at the palace, resistance was crushed within three hours. Eventually Diem and Nhu escaped from the palace through a secret tunnel and hid in Cholon, the Chinese section of Saigon. On the morning of 2 November, having been promised safe conduct out of the country, they were instead tracked down and summarily shot to death in the back of an armoured personnel carrier.

With Diem dead US policy in Vietnam had to be re-defined. Another result of his death was that people could at last tell the truth about how badly the war was going for the government. Even Lodge, who was expecting bad news, was shocked at how discouraging it was. On 21 November he left for Washington to inform the President that the situation was much worse than they had thought. At San Francisco he learned that John Kennedy had been shot dead at Dallas. The Vietnam War had become the responsibility of Lyndon Johnson.

Six

JOHNSON'S WAR

Lodge's revelations about the failure of the Strategic Hamlets Programme and the ineffectiveness of the counter-insurgency campaign produced an uncompromising response from the new American President. 'I am not,' affirmed Johnson, 'going to lose Vietnam.' Nor did he intend to allow Southeast Asia 'go the way China went'.[1] Within four days of taking office he confirmed US support for Diem's successors and requested plans for clandestine operations against the government in the North.[2] In December he reviewed the whole situation as presented in a report from McNamara who had returned from a visit to Vietnam with a belatedly realistic appraisal of the war.

McNamara, still Secretary of Defense, found the new government in Saigon inexperienced and indecisive and that the US establishment there was functioning badly, partly as a result of tensions between Lodge and Harkins. The enemy, on the other hand, had, since the death of Diem, grown even more formidable. The Vietcong dominated a number of key provinces where they had destroyed many strategic hamlets and replaced government officials with their own men who 'collected taxes at will'. McNamara advised the President to run scared, 'hoping for the best, but preparing for more forceful moves'.[3] In January the Joint Chiefs of Staff urged him to increase the pressure on the enemy, arguing that the Vietnam War was assuming global significance and that the United States should no longer pull any punches. While welcoming the proposed covert actions against the North, they warned that a much higher 'level of activity' was necessary to impress both friend and foe.[4] A greater degree of American control and more extensive action against North Vietnam were two of their proposals which were soon implemented. Meanwhile the elaborate programme of clandestine actions against the North, code-named Operation Plan 34A, began on 1 February.

12. Members of the South Vietnamese 'Popular Force' on patrol in a strategic hamlet.

Included in the programme, which was of course concealed from the public, were U-2 spy-plane flights over North Vietnam, kidnapping North Vietnamese for intelligence information, dropping sabotage teams to blow up rail and road bridges and bombarding coastal installations from PT boats. The operations were planned by the US and Saigon authorities and carried out by South Vietnamese or 'hired personnel' (Asian mercenaries). Control of the whole plan lay in the hands of General Harkins. At the same time, destroyer patrols, code-named De Soto patrols, began to collect information about North Vietnamese radar and coastal defences in the Gulf of Tonkin. Yet another measure was an intensification of air operations in Laos, one of Vietnam's western neighbours.

The purpose of all such activity was to tighten the pressure on the leaders of North Vietnam. It was hoped that they in turn would seek relief by exerting their influence on the NLF to end the insurgency in the South. Rostow, chairman of the State Department Policy Planning Council, and one of the government's leading intellectuals, argued that the revolution in the South could be 'dried up' by cutting off its external sources of support and supply.[5] Thus when it became evident that the 34A operations were having little effect, the possible bombing of the North appeared on the agenda, although almost a year elapsed before full-scale attacks were launched. The way was, as we shall see, carefully prepared before the big decision was taken. However, while there was some agonizing over issues of timing and possible international consequences, there was virtually no questioning of the main 'justification' for a bombing offensive – that the North was responsible for the war in the South.

The presumption of Northern guilt was clear in the National Security Council memorandum agreed by Johnson on 26 November 1963. In order to defend the new measures against the North it directed the State Department to produce a documented case 'to demonstrate to the world the degree to which the Viet Cong is controlled, sustained and supplied from Hanoi'.[6] Eventually, in February 1965, State published a White Paper making the allegations used to justify US bombing. 'In Viet Nam,' it declared, 'a Communist government has set out deliberately to conquer a sovereign people in a neighbouring state.'[7] The authors had, however, some difficulty in finding convincing evidence for their accusation. One, who was responsible for gathering proof of infiltration from the North, later commented that the document was a 'dismal disappointment' and that 'the actual findings seemed pretty frail'.[8] Not only were they pretty frail, they were contradicted by other American sources, even by the State Department itself. In June 1964 its Director of Intelligence pointed out that not only were most of the Vietcong South Vietnamese but also that most of their weapons came not from communist countries but from capture, purchase or local manufacture.[9] The failure of the White Paper to make its case was immediately publicized in a detailed reply to it written by an independent journalist, I. F. Stone.[10] Subsequently, information in the Pentagon Papers undermined other arguments which attempted to justify the bombing campaign.

One such argument was advanced, after the US had already escalated the war, by Secretary of State Rusk. He claimed, in a Senate Hearing, that the North Vietnamese had moved their 325th Division into South Vietnam before the bombing started.[11] The Pentagon analyst, however, has shown that, when the order to bomb was finally issued in February 1965, the US knew of no regular Northern military units in the South.[12] Rusk, like the President and other policy makers, had the facility of ignoring facts which clashed with their own preconceptions. To manufacture acceptable reasons for the US bombing it was necessary to believe that they were responding to intolerable pressure from the other side. The fact that the evidence for such pressure was insubstantial was simply ignored.

However, the Johnson administration had not merely to convince themselves that escalation was necessary. They also had to prepare the American people for a significant and costly extension of the war effort in Southeast Asia. In fact they had to be educated to accept that events had transformed the war from one in which Vietnamese could be left to fight each other, with the US supporting the 'good' Vietnamese, into a conflict which demanded direct participation by the United States. During the last decade Vietnam has been such a dominant issue in American politics that it takes an effort to recall that in 1964 it was only one of many issues. Few Americans outside government circles knew what was happening in Vietnam. Even fewer were anxious to increase the US commitment there. The major topic in 1964 was the Presidential election and the indications were that most Americans wanted a president who would not embroil them in a major war in Asia. A convincing victory in the election was Johnson's principal concern. Every issue was to be handled with that objective in mind – including the issue of Vietnam. The President required McNamara 'to keep Vietnam in hand and tidy it up'.[13] Within the administration discussion of the war was limited; only the very top people were involved in the decisions.

The tenor of the confidential debate was that a more forceful US policy should be pursued in Vietnam at 'an appropriate moment'. All the major policy makers agreed with McNamara's statement of US objectives in South Vietnam. In effect he postulated the right of the USA to defeat the revolution there by 'economic and social pressures' together with 'police and military help'. He claimed that the conflict was seen by the rest of the world as a 'test case of US capacity to help a nation meet a Communist "war of liberation"'.[14] There was no doubting the terrible consequences of American failure. Vietnam, Laos and Cambodia would probably be dominated by 'Communism'. Obliged to 'accommodate to Communism', Burma would cease to be an American sphere of influence. Thailand would soon be under pressure. The Philippines would become vulnerable and the 'threat' would be greatly increased to the following: India, Australia and New Zealand, Taiwan, Korea and Japan.[15]

McNamara's memorandum, so specific in some respects, revealed considerable confusion as to who the enemy was and about the precise nature of the threat. Was he referring to Soviet Communism, Chinese Communism or the Communism of North Vietnam? Which brand threatened which country? Was he contending, for example, that New Zealand was menaced by the North Vietnamese? There was a question also regarding the definition of a 'Communist war of liberation'. Such a war, according to the view from the Left, was one in which indigenous revolutionaries were in conflict with the established government of a country and its imperial protectors. McNamara's document implied that it was a war in which an external Communist power (North Vietnam in this case) imposed a Communist regime on another country with the help of a fifth column (the Vietcong).

Since 1945 American leaders had constantly invoked the menace of an international Communist conspiracy directed from Moscow and, after 1949, also from Peking. In the wake of the Sino–Soviet split that particular (but unparticularized) threat ceased to be credible. What remained was a scarcely identifiable adversary, a rather mysterious but dangerous force, difficult to specify in any concrete terms.[16] From the memorandum it is, however, possible to deduce why that vague force could cause such perturbation in Washington. Clearly, McNamara believed that it threatened to undermine the influence of the United States, denying to the Americans their 'right' to apply economic and military pressure to maintain their dominant status in the world, their 'super-powerdom'. While the precise nature of the international communist enemy was rather conjectural the US response was definite enough: a massive military commitment in Southeast Asia.

The North Vietnamese were identified as the most urgent danger to US dominance and preparations were made to deal with them when the right moment came or could be contrived. In April the Joint Chiefs of Staff approved a plan for 'retaliatory' (sic) air-strikes within 72 hours and for full-scale bombing of the North on 30 days' notice. The plan stated how many planes and what bomb tonnages would be required and provided a list of targets with the damage to be inflicted. At the same time an estimate was made of possible Chinese and North Vietnamese reactions, together with the number of American ground forces needed to cope with them. The air-war scenario specified that on D-Day − 30 there should be a 'Presidential speech in general terms launching [a] Joint Resolution' [of Congress].[17] William Bundy, Assistant Secretary of State for Far Eastern Affairs, in fact drafted the Congressional resolution on 25 May – the resolution which was finally put to Congress in August, after the Gulf of Tonkin incident.[18]

It was considered inappropriate to tell the Congress or the American people how much was being done for their protection. Johnson eagerly anticipated contending against Barry Goldwater in the November election when he would present himself as the reasonable man of the centre, the master of consensus politics, against the wild man of the Republican right. Goldwater exposed himself to attack because of his bellicose attitudes. While he did not actually advocate nuclear war, he talked so much about it that he appeared as an irresponsible war-monger. He did in fact favour an air-war against North Vietnam. To gain maximum leverage from Goldwater's bellicosity, Johnson had to conceal

13. **Phom Van Dong, North Vietnamese prime minister, with British journalist James Cameron in Hanoi.**

the fact that he himself was preparing to bomb the North. He did so very effectively and was publicly proclaimed as the peace candidate while privately making cautious but definite steps towards a wider war.

In June the administration implemented one of the proposals

in the April air-war scenario: that an intermediary should tell Hanoi that the US was determined to protect South Vietnam. Seaborn, the Canadian representative on the International Control Commission, secretly met the North Vietnamese Prime Minister at the request of the US government. He informed Pham Van Dong that American patience was not limitless. The United States 'knew' the control exercised by the North over the Vietcong and warned that any escalation by the Vietcong would result in 'the greatest devastation' of North Vietnam itself.[19] Disregarding that warning, the guerrillas persisted, with great success, in attacking the military regime in Saigon. With an intemperance born of despair General Khanh, the South Vietnamese leader, boasted publicly that he would invade the North. The US felt obliged to reassure its demoralized ally. On 24 July Khanh was told confidentially that the Americans might themselves attack the North if the pressure on his government became excessive.[20] The Joint Chiefs in fact proposed air strikes against the North by unmarked planes flown by non-American crews. Before their proposal could be considered it was overtaken by events.

On 31 July South Vietnamese naval commandos, part of the 34A programme, attacked the North Vietnamese islands Hon Me and Hon Nieu in the Gulf of Tonkin. Shortly afterwards, on 2 August, the US destroyer *Maddox*, which was engaged on a De Soto intelligence gethering patrol, was attacked by North Vietnamese torpedo boats. Two were damaged by planes from the nearby aircraft-carrier *Ticonderoga*, the third was sunk by the *Maddox*. Johnson, on 3 August, ordered the *Maddox*, supported by another destroyer the *C. Turner Joy*, to return to the Tonkin Gulf. A second carrier, the *Constellation*, joined the *Ticonderoga*. During the night of 4 August both destroyers signalled that they were under attack. Because of the Pacific time-difference, news of the incident reached Washington in mid-morning on the 4th. By 1.25 p.m. the Chiefs of Staff had recommended that fighter-bombers from *Ticonderoga* and *Constellation* should retaliate by attacking four North Vietnamese torpedo-boat bases and an oil-storage depot. Having approved the raids, Johnson met Congressional leaders from both parties to outline the day's events and to request a resolution approving his policy. They promised support for what the President had described as a 'limited retaliation'. While the aircraft were heading for their targets Johnson informed the American people on television that the actions taken had been a 'fitting' response which accorded with 'the highest tradition of the United States Navy'.[21]

The next day McNamara reported that twenty-five North Vietnamese patrol craft had been destroyed or damaged, as had 90 per cent of the oil storage tanks near Vinh. It remained to produce a post-facto 'justification' for the damage. The Congressional resolution (drafted, as we have seen, by the administration) approved and supported the determination of the President to 'take all necessary measures to repel any armed attack against the forces of the United States and to prevent further aggression'. It went on to declare that the US regarded international peace and security in Southeast Asia as vital to its national interest. Therefore the USA was prepared 'as the President determines', to take any action 'including the use of armed force, to assist any member or protocol state of the Southeast Asia Collective Defense Treaty requiring assistance in defense of its freedom'.[22] McNamara and Rusk testified on behalf of the resolution in secret sessions of the Senate and House of Representatives Foreign Relations Committee on 6 August. On the following day it was passed in the Senate by 88 votes to 2 and in the House by 416 to 0.

As the voting figures indicate, there were few Americans who questioned their government's policy at that time. Senator Wayne Morse, one of the two dissentients, did indeed beg Fulbright, the chairman of the Senate Foreign Relations Committee, to hold genuine hearings on the resolution and warned that its wording was too general and too open-ended for any president, especially President Johnson.[23] Subsequently it became clear that Morse and Gruening, the other opposer, were totally justified in their opposition. The US government had, it emerged, played a gigantic confidence trick on Congress and the American people.

In the first place it was exceedingly doubtful whether there had been any attack on 4 August. Captain John Herrick, commander of the Tonkin Gulf patrol, had signalled to the Pentagon: 'Review of action makes reported contacts and torpedoes fired appear doubtful. Freak weather reports and over-eager sonar men may have accounted for many reports. No actual sightings by *Maddox*. Suggest complete evaluation before further action.' Senator Fulbright, who was responsible for piloting the resolution through the Senate Foreign Relations Committee, later commented about Herrick's report: 'If I had known of that one telegram, if that had been put before me . . . I certainly don't think I would have rushed into action.'[24] Although they knew that visibility was bad ('blacker than the hubs of Hell') and that no US ship had sustained any damage, the Pentagon, after a perfunctory inquiry into Herrick's doubts, decided that there had been an attack by the North Vietnamese. Some months later, however, President Johnson, commenting on the Tonkin incident, remarked with a grin: 'For all I know, our Navy was shooting at whales out there.'[25]

Whether or not there had been an attack, the retaliatory air strikes could hardly be justified since there had been so much provocation of the North. While the 34A attacks had been generally ineffectual, they had given the enemy good reason for launching retaliatory strikes of their own. Herrick, having intercepted North Vietnamese radio traffic, realized that the enemy considered his destroyer patrol to be part of the operation that had attacked North Vietnamese installations on 31 July. When the *Maddox* was ordered, on 3 August, to return to the Gulf he warned that the continuance of the patrol was 'an unacceptable risk'.[26] It was undoubtedly an additional provocation. At the secret hearings on 6 August Morse questioned McNamara about the 34A raids and the connection between them and the destroyer patrol. McNamara lied to the senators, claiming that the US Navy had been unaware of any South Vietnamese actions and that the *Maddox* had been simply carrying out a routine patrol 'of the type we carry out all over the world at all times'.[27] Quite unscrupulously the Johnson administration turned the truth on its head, alleging that the US had been provoked by North Vietnam. Faced with such 'provocation' they beat the patriotic drum and almost all Americans fell in behind the flag. Eventually a price was paid for such sharp practice – widespread disillusionment. Fulbright, for example, was to comment later: 'I regret it more than anything I have ever done in my life, that I was the vehicle which took the resolution to the floor.'[28]

The Johnson administration was not the first to hoodwink Congress and the people, nor was it the last. Covert operations had been a feature of Kennedy's government: the Watergate affair has revealed some of the manipulations of the Nixon era. Even so, the Tonkin Gulf affair is worth particular attention. It was in the short-run so successful – a prime example of how the executive branch could manipulate the legislature and public opinion. The pattern was set for the rest of Johnson's term of office. The insiders simply assumed that they knew best; they would protect the people simultaneously from 'communism' and the truth. Hence the devious launching of the air-war, the build-up of ground troops, the covert operations against Laos, the undermining of any attempts to negotiate a settlement and so on and so on. Yet while they were diddling others, they were also deluding themselves. The Tonkin events left the President and his lieutenants with the illusion that they knew how to deal with North Vietnam.[29] They convinced themselves that they could achieve results by force, the use of which they could carefully regulate. In fact what they produced in August was a temporary success which involved the USA even more deeply in a war which was soon to get completely out of control. They managed to fool everyone except the enemy.

On the domestic front, it is true, Johnson continued to fool most of the people long enough to win handsomely in the elections. Between August and November he played alternately Dr Jekyll and Mr Hyde. In public he opposed widening the conflict and so being forced to send American boys to a war that 'ought to be fought by the boys of Asia'.[30] Less than two weeks after voicing those sentiments he approved preparations for extending the war in Laos. At the same time he indicated his readiness to take 'larger decisions' when necessary. The Pentagon analyst considered that by September there was a consensus in the government that 'overt military operations' against North Vietnam would begin in the new year.[31]

The Vietcong provided an occasion for one larger decision on 1 November, two days before the Presidential election. In a mortar attack on Bienhoa, an airfield near Saigon, they killed four Americans, destroyed five B-57 bombers and damaged eight others. The 'provocation' was greater than during the Tonkin Gulf incident and the Joint Chiefs favoured 'a prompt and strong response'.[32] Johnson decided to do nothing and his caution was well rewarded when on 3 November he gained his desired landslide victory over Goldwater.

With victory on the home front achieved the President was able to expedite preparations for an enlarged war. At the beginning of December he approved a two-phase bombing plan. Phase 1 involved 'reprisal' air-strikes and intensifying unpublicized attacks against the enemy. It was to be followed by Phase 2 – a sustained air-war against North Vietnam. On 10 December the Prime Minister of Laos agreed to US air-strikes against part of the Ho Chi Minh Trail, one of the supply lines between North and South Vietnam which ran through Laos. Such attacks, code-named Operation Barrell Roll, were part of Phase 1. There was to be no statement about the use of American planes unless one were lost. In that case the administration would claim that US aircraft were escorting reconnaissance flights 'as requested by the Laotian government'.[33] In January 1965, after the loss of two US jets, information about air operations in Laos began to filter through the security screen. Senator Morse, one of a small minority which took seriously press speculation that the US might be preparing to strike the North, condemned the air activity that had been taking place over Laos since 1964. The rule of law, he stated, had been replaced by the jungle law of military might. He predicted that unless US policy towards Southeast Asia changed there would be no hope of avoiding 'a massive war in Asia'.[34] As with the Tonkin resolution, Morse was later proved right. At the time he was ignored and the only change in American policy was to carry out the long-threatened bombing of North Vietnam.

It was finally precipitated by a mortar attack on 6 February against a United States contingent at Pleiku in which nine Americans were killed and seventy-six wounded. Within fourteen hours 49 US Navy jets had loosed their bombs and rockets on the North Vietnamese base at Donghoi. After a further Vietcong attack on an American barracks at Quinhon, Johnson ordered a second, heavier, reprisal raid on 11 February. Two days later he decided to launch Operation Rolling Thunder – the sustained air-war against North Vietnam.[35]

The consequences of US bombing in Indochina are examined in some detail in the next chapter. Here we might note briefly that there were many civilian casualties in the North, despite American claims that military targets could be destroyed with minimum loss of civilian life. Such casualties had exactly the opposite effect of that intended by Johnson's generals. They had urged bombing the North to coerce Ho's government to stop helping the insurgents in the South. In fact, however, Operation Rolling Thunder sharpened the spirit of resistance. James Cameron has pointed out that, 'From the moment the United States dropped its first bomb on the North of Vietnam, she welded the nation together unshakeably. Every bomb since was a bonus for Ho Chi Minh.'[36] Equally ineffective was the attempt to disrupt the economy. It was, as Cameron again noted, an immensely resilient peasant society, not easily wrecked by high-explosives. 'Every single industrial enterprise in the country could be ruined – and it would directly effect about 5 percent of the working population.'[37]

At the same time as it began its highly publicized attacks on the North, the US also launched an intensive air-war in South Vietnam. We consider later its full impact; it is appropriate at this point to observe that it was even more destructive than the bombing north of the seventeenth parallel. To the south of the line the US Air Force accomplished wholesale destruction of the land and its peasant population. By forcing millions of peasants to seek the safety of refugee camps – despite their appalling living conditions – the Americans did hurt the enemy. In a guerrilla war the peasants are the sea and the guerrillas the fish; if the sea can be dried up the fish die. On the other hand, the devastation increased hostility to the United States and their South Vietnamese allies. During the first year of bombing in the South Vietcong recruitment tripled.[38]

Even when the bombing was intensified enemy morale stayed high. Between 1965 and 1969 both North and South Vietnam were subjected to an incredible bombardment from the air. In that time about 4.5 million tons were dropped – 'over 70 tons of bombs for every square mile of Vietnam, North and South . . . about 500 pounds of bombs for every man, woman and child in Vietnam'.[39] Even that staggering demonstration of the US capacity for destruction was not enough to bring Johnson his victory.

The unlikelihood of the bombers delivering a crushing blow was appreciated early in the campaign. Indeed the air-war had scarcely begun before the military, realizing that it would produce no quick solution, were pressing for more ground troops in Vietnam. On 8 March 3,500 marines disembarked at Danang to protect its air base. At the end of the month the US Commander-in-Chief, Westmoreland, advised that the South Vietnamese army needed American reinforcements to 'hold the line'. On 1 April Johnson, so adamant a few months earlier about 'Asian boys' doing their own fighting, decided to use American ground troops for

'It says: "Sorry, but programming omitted factor of human spirit."

14.

offensive action in South Vietnam. It was a drastic departure from previous policy and meant American involvement in another major land war in Asia. The President characteristically attempted to conceal the change from the public and it was not until 8 June that it 'crept out almost by accident in a State Department release . . .'[40] He was equally secretive when he announced on 28 July his decision to increase the number of US troops from 75,000 to 125,000. The fact was that he had decided that the American troop level in Vietnam would be 175,000 as a minimum and might reach the figure of 200,000. Thus the President carried out a major escalation of the war and, at the same time, a major deception on the American people. (Halberstam suggests that this point was the real beginning of the credibility gap.[41]) At the end of 1965 US forces in Vietnam numbered 184,000.[42]

The escalation and the deception continued in subsequent years. In February 1966, by which time the troops' total was 235,000, Johnson announced: 'We do not have on my desk at the moment any unfilled requests from General Westmoreland.'[43] In fact, Westmoreland had demanded, at the end of January, a total of 459,000. By September 1966 he had 325,000 of them; however he estimated that for 1967 he would require 542,500. In August 1967 Johnson agreed to a total of 525,000. Following the enemy's Tet offensive of February 1968 Westmoreland argued for a further

200,000 men to raise the total to more than 700,000. Thereupon Johnson finally called a halt: at the end of March he rebuffed his generals with a 'token' increase of some 20,000 men. Three years after launching his bombers and his battalions he recognized that victory had eluded him.

The American commander during those years, General Westmoreland, was an orthodox career soldier – 'his background was conventional war, and both his instincts and responses were conventional'.[44] His policy at first was to establish firm bases, whence he could strike the enemy. During 1966 he used small mobile groups to attack Vietcong concentrations: a tactic thwarted by the enemy's superior intelligence service. As his numbers and material increased he built up large, superbly equipped, multi-divisional forces with elaborate air support. They carried out huge 'search and destroy' missions which killed many Vietnamese but failed to deliver a decisive blow against the Vietcong. The enemy soldiers they killed were quickly replaced; one official commented that they were fighting Vietnam's birth-rate.[45] General Depuy, Westmoreland's chief strategist, thought that the answer was 'more bombs, more shells, more napalm . . . till the other side cracks and gives up'.[46] It did neither. Despite all Westmoreland's efforts the Vietcong were able to mass enough forces to launch a major offensive which helped to convince Johnson that a military victory was not possible in Vietnam.

On 31 January 1968, the period of the New Year (Tet) in Vietnam, between 50,000 and 60,000 Vietcong, with the co-operation of hundreds of thousands of urban residents, occupied most of the populated areas in South Vietnam. Even the US Embassy in Saigon was captured and held for some 24 hours. Hué, the principal city in central Vietnam, was occupied until the offensive petered out, under devastating American bombardment, at the end of February. By that time the guerrillas had attacked 34 provincial centres, 64 district towns and most cities of any size. Attempts were made to play down the Tet offensive: the VC, it was claimed, had sustained crippling losses. From the Pentagon history, however, it is clear that the offensive had caught the US leaders unawares and that 'its strength, length and intensity prolonged this shock'.[47]

At the end of February Johnson ordered a complete review of American policy in Vietnam. Clark Clifford, soon to replace

McNamara as Secretary of Defense, convened a group of senior advisers which presented a memorandum in favour of curtailing the war. It contended that even if a further 200,000 troops were deployed, as Westmoreland wished, the US would still be unable to win the war. Hanoi, it argued, had enough reserves to match a further American commitment. Also, if the US continued to pour more and more resources into the war, it would become difficult to convince critics that they were not in fact destroying Vietnam in order to 'save' it from Communism. Such a continued diversion of resources would also accentuate the discontent of those who felt that urgent domestic problems were being neglected as a result of the war. There was a serious risk, warned Clifford's group, of provoking 'a domestic crisis of unprecedented proportions.'[48]

Despite the opposition of his generals, the President, as already noted, did check the flow of troops to Vietnam. In a crucial speech on 31 March he announced the 'token' increase of 20,000. At the same time he declared that further attacks on North Vietnam by US aircraft and Navy vessels would be limited to an area north of the demilitarized zone. Thus the area exempted from bombing contained nearly 90 per cent of the population and almost all the territory of the North. All the major populated centres were to be spared further attack.[49] At the end of his speech Johnson, having reduced the bombing 12,000 miles away, dropped a bombshell on Washington. He withdrew from the Presidential election of 1968.

We consider subsequently how public opinion turned against Johnson's handling of the war. It was recognition of their disillusionment that persuaded him to renounce his hope of re-election. After his withdrawal he was virtually powerless to make any conclusive move on Vietnam. He had to some degree limited the escalation of the war but did not have the political status, far less the personal inclination, to bring it to an end. On 3 April he announced that Hanoi was ready to meet US representatives to discuss the issues. Thereafter the war dragged on, as did the campaign to elect a new President. Johnson's war was virtually over: Nixon's was still to come.

Seven

THE DEVASTATION OF VIETNAM

It took some time for ordinary Americans to appreciate the impact of the US presence in Vietnam. They were told repeatedly by their leaders that their objective was the independence of South Vietnam. Shortly after the escalation in the spring of 1965 Johnson had explained that Americans wanted nothing for themselves. They would use their power with restraint not only to protect South Vietnam's freedom but also to help all countries of Southeast Asia. The task was nothing less than to 'enrich the hopes and existence of more than a hundred million people'.[1] Such stressing of America's constructive purpose in Vietnam was for a time highly functional. The administration was able to prosecute the war with the idealistic backing of most Americans. On the other hand, when the truth emerged, the shock was all the greater. The truth was that Indochina had been devastated by its *soi-disant* defenders.

In 1968, when the nature of the war had become apparent, one British observer wrote: 'America protects the freedom of the Vietnamese by helicopters armed with batteries of machine-guns, which spray entire villages with bullets and "flush out" – the clean, antiseptic military phrase – their inhabitants; by cumbersome, big-bellied aircraft which, every week, pour hundreds of tons of herbicides on growing crops. They drop steel-blades . . . by the thousand and clusters of steel balls, the size of hand grenades, which break on impact and scatter lethal pellets through the thin partitions of the peasants' huts. In Vietnam the treasures of the American way of death are spread out as in a shop-window.'[2]

The point has been very often made that the Americans sought to achieve 'liberation' by means of destruction. If we remember another equally obvious point, that the guerrillas were largely indistinguishable from the other peasants and lived among them, we can appreciate that the destruction of the Vietcong necessarily entailed the devastation of the villages and the death of the villagers. In the Vietnam war there were usually no conventional military fronts and no areas where guerrilla influence was wholly eradicated. From the American standpoint the front line was everywhere and everyone was potentially the enemy.

Those realities had determined the conduct of the conflict even before its intensification in 1965. Under Diem there had been a virtual war against the peasants. In December 1962 the State Department intelligence section noted that extensive use of artillery and aerial bombardment by the South Vietnamese government, in its attempts to eliminate the guerrillas, had 'killed many innocent peasants and made many others more willing than before to co-operate with the Viet Cong'.[3] Even in this early stage the casualties were appalling. The French authority, Bernard Fall, estimated that 89,000 Vietcong had been killed between 1961 and April 1965.[4] Given the indiscriminate bombardment of whole areas where there were no easily definable military targets, civilian casualties were generally very high.

Until 1965 South Vietnamese peasants had suffered largely at the hands of their 'own' air force.[5] From February of that year they had to contend also with the US Air Force. As already noted, it was then that the long-pondered decision to bomb the North was taken. In April, however, it was decided that, in the use of American air power, priority should be given to South Vietnam. By May large areas had been designated 'free bombing zones' where 'tens of thousands of tons of bombs, rockets, napalm and cannon fire' were poured in every week.[6] In June, Johnson authorized raids on South Vietnam by huge B-52 bombers with a standard load of fifty-one 750-pound bombs of high explosive or many more incendiary bombs. Operating from Guam or Thailand, they attacked from 30,000 to 40,000 feet, too high to be seen or heard. They blasted and burned large areas of jungle, roads, buildings, fields and, of course, people.[7] One American study found, not surprisingly, that B-52s were 'the most devastating and frightening weapons used so far against the VC'.[8] As the war persisted the bombing increased, from 315,000 tons in 1965 to 1,388,000 tons in 1969.[9]

Bombardment from the air was only one aspect of the 'unparalleled, lavish use of firepower as a substitute for manpower' which, according to a Pentagon official, was the main feature of American tactics in Vietnam.[10] Artillery bombardment was more frequent and may have been even more destructive. Ground ammunition expended increased from 577,000 tons in 1966 to 1,374,000 tons in 1969. In 1968 and 1969 the US was using about 7,700 to 7,800 tons of ground and air ordnance in an average day – about 500 times the quantity used by the NLF forces.[12] Those statistics indicate how the scale of war enlarged and say something about the great disparity of resources between the two sides. The extent of the destruction they represent can, however, scarcely be conceived. For any picture of it to emerge the figures must be supplemented with accounts of a land pock-marked with bomb craters, of charred fields, forests where trees could not be felled since they were full of shell fragments.[13] The successes of lavish firepower require to be measured in terms of fields, where rice once grew, being submerged in sea-water following the bombing of a dike; of the hills overlooking the flooded rice fields being 'ironed' – a term used by the peasants to indicate that they were riddled with bomb fragments, mines and unexploded artillery shells.[14] Another index of American technological achievement was that South Vietnam, which until 1964 was an exporter of rice, became, after 1965, a heavy rice importer.

Crop destruction was achieved not only by bombardment but also by chemical warfare. Defoliation of trees to facilitate the detection of guerrillas had been approved by Kennedy in 1962.[15] Known as Operation Ranch Hand, the programme was carried out by a group flying C-123 aircraft whose slogan was 'Only We Can Prevent Forests'.[16] The defoliation programme was supplemented by an anti-crop project and by the end of 1966 more than half the C-123 missions were targeted against crops.[17] In July 1966 the *New York Times* revealed that, since 1962, the spraying had blighted some 130,000 acres of rice and other food plants.[18] During the next few years chemical warfare expanded rapidly. In the first nine months of 1967 defoliants were sprayed on 843,606 acres and crop-killing chemicals on another 121,400 acres. The US Air Force estimated an expenditure of $70.8 million on destructive chemicals in the year 1968–9, an increase of $24.9 million over the previous year.[19] An American authority commented in May 1968 that, while the long-term effects of spraying were imponderable, the short-term results were certain: leaves, trees, rice plants and other vegetation were dead or dying: many insects, birds and animals and some human beings also had either migrated or died of starvation. The North Vietnamese were, he commented, fortunate – they had only bombs to contend with.[20]

The various methods of destruction employed by the US in Vietnam were very costly and took a good deal of organizing; there was nothing haphazard about them. Their purpose was, as the American authorities have acknowledged often enough, to eliminate the guerrillas. Since the guerrillas were embedded in the peasant society, their elimination involved the destruction of that society. It was not possible to undertake such a task without killing many innocent people. In practice that was what happened. Naturally enough US military spokesmen and apologists have tried to uphold the fiction that they did their best not to harm non-combatants. They have had an uphill struggle against a mountain of evidence that in Vietnam the indiscriminate killing of civilians was as American as cherry pie.

A few random examples may be cited. Charles Mohr, Saigon correspondent of the *New York Times*, reported on 5 September 1965: 'This is strategic bombing in a friendly, allied country. Since the Vietcong doctrine is to insulate themselves among the population and the population is powerless to prevent their presence, no one here seriously doubts that significant numbers of innocent civilians are dying every day in South Viet-Nam.'[21] Another *Times* reporter, Jack Langguth, commented on official attempts to cover up such facts. On one occasion the US authorities claimed that the victims of an air strike were Vietcong soldiers. Having investigated the incident Langguth discovered that 'three out of four patients seeking treatment in a Vietnamese hospital afterward for burns from napalm or jellied gasoline were village women'.[22] The military were not always so secretive. A Lieutenant-Colonel who introduced a French journalist, Jean Bertolino, to his immediate superior volunteered the information that the General hunted the Vietcong with a rifle from his Iroquois helicopter. The General shrugged off Bertolino's comment that surely it was not possible from the air to distinguish the Vietcong from civilians.[23]

Katsuichi Honda, a Japanese journalist, once found himself at the receiving end of helicopter fire: 'They seemed to fire whimsically . . . even though they were not being shot at from the ground nor could they identify the people as NLF. They did it impulsively for fun, using the farmers for targets as if in a hunting

mood. They are hunting Asians.'[24] American soldiers have themselves contributed to the evidence: a helicopter gunner has claimed
that he was ordered to kill unarmed civilians; a medic has testified
that some twenty-seven civilians at a peaceful meeting were
killed by US tanks firing 'a barrage of tiny arrow-like nails'.[25]
Many other examples could be quoted *ad nauseam*.

Orders involving attacks on civilians emanated from the very
top. Neil Sheehan, compiler of the *New York Times* edition of the
Pentagon Papers, has claimed that the 'highest level of authority
in Saigon' vetoed a suggestion that the policy of unrestricted
bombing and shelling should be reconsidered. The authority held
fast to the idea of defeating the Vietnamese Communists 'by oblit-
erating their strategic base, the rural population'.[26] We might note
that from the Pentagon Papers it is clear that the President and his
policy makers had no illusions about its consequences when they
authorized the campaign against the rural society in South
Vietnam.[27] Against such a background, the massacre at My Lai,
which produced world-wide reactions of shock and horror,
appears simply as one more incident in a saga of indiscriminate
violence.[28]

Apart from causing wholesale devastation and innumerable
casualties, the bombs, shells, napalm, chemicals, mines and so on
were successful in 'generating' many refugees. That was the
euphemism for uprooting millions of peasants from their villages
and penning them in camps where they could no longer give
support to the NLF. The forced evacuation of the peasantry caused
problems for the guerrillas but was not sufficient to eliminate them.
It did however cause great misery. There is no accurate figure for
the refugees 'generated' during Johnson's war: estimates vary from
two million to four million. In any case they were a substantial
proportion of the whole population. Their living conditions were
exceedingly bad. Mary McCarthy, the novelist, visited one camp
where a stagnant duck-pond provided the only water for 700
people to drink, wash and cook. Another duck-pond, slightly
larger, supplied the remaining 800 inhabitants. 'There were,' she
noted, 'no sanitary facilities of any kind; we saw women and
children squatting; garbage was strewn in front of the huts, which
had earth floors and inflammable old straw roofing.'[29] Senator
Edward Kennedy inspected some camps where thousands of people
were 'literally starving to death'. He revealed that the annual

15. **President Nguyen Van Thieu.**

expenditure on the refugee programme was less than the amount spent by the US on the war in half a day.[30]

The refugee situation, like every other problem, was completely mishandled by the South Vietnamese government. Ostensibly – we may recall – the US aspired to ensure that the people of South Vietnam had an efficient and democratic government. In fact it was neither. Between 1964 and 1967 the military hierarchy played musical chairs for the political leadership of the country. In 1964 Nguyen Khanh staged a coup against Diem's successors. He himself was 'neurotic, paranoiac, disliked by both older officers and younger officers, and like his predecessors, totally overwhelmed by the political problems he faced'.[31] Of the numerous other figures who emerged to succeed him we might mention the two most prominent. Nguyen Cao Ky, a young adventurer whose hero was, he proudly proclaimed, Adolf Hitler, was Prime Minister from 1965 to 1967. In that year he was relegated to the post of Vice-President by his rival Nguyen Van Thieu who became President. Thieu was to provide stability of a kind in that he managed to keep himself in power. His regime had the durability of Diem's. Also like Diem's, and every other South Vietnamese government, it was corrupt, repressive, totally dependent on US support and ineffectual in dealing with the major problems of a society convulsed by a devastating war.

Instances abound of peculation and malversation in South Vietnamese governments.[32] Fitzgerald has described how in 1966 Ky and Thieu made the arrangements necessary to support 'a new and more stable system of corruption'. The generals commanding the First and Second Corps were allowed to enrich themselves through military preferments and disposing of US commodities; the Fourth Corps commander traded in rice and opium; the Defence Minister flourished by means of property deals. Thieu put his financial transactions into the efficient, diamond-bedecked hands of his wife. Ky – more concerned with power than mere personal enrichment – used the money that came his way to buy provincial officials and to hire his own band of thugs.[33] One of the most serious forms of corruption, in an allegedly democratic country, is the rigging of elections. The evidence suggests that every election in South Vietnam has been rigged. Having examined the 1967 election, for example, Lederer concluded that the Thieu–Ky regime was not backed by the people; that it had to resort to bribery, terror and disqualification of unfriendly voters to stay in power. He considered that the regime was 'afraid of the democratic process'.[34]

Fearing the democratic process, the cliques who have governed South Vietnam have simply avoided it. After the fall of Diem even official Washington admitted how repressive his regime had been. Similar repression continued after 1963 and was constantly condoned by the United States. In September 1968, Professor Ly Chanh Trung, a prominent South Vietnamese Catholic intellectual, declared: '. . . the inhabitants of the southern part of Viet Nam have not been able to enjoy freedom, and have not had the chance to be masters of their own destiny, precisely because the Americans, in

the name of the protectors of freedom, have, in fact, been protecting regimes which stamp out that freedom.'[35] The successors of
Diem have used his methods: suppression of newspapers; banning
opposition groups; maintaining camps for political prisoners – and
so on. A limitation of political freedom is specifically included in
the 1967 constitution, of which Article V states: 'The Republic
of Viet-Nam opposes communism in every form. Every activity
designed to propagandize or carry out communism is prohibited.'[36]
Non-communist opponents of the military juntas appreciated that
communism was a category that could be extended to include, for
example, Buddhists.[37]

Like Diem, the generals used the apparatus of oppression and
rigged elections principally in order to stay where they were. The
ultimate corruption of the Saigon regimes was their complete
egocentrism. Their corruption was not a falling away from an
ideal, since they had no ideals; even their anti-communism was a
dogma of convenience, a key to America's treasure-chest. While
even Diem had possessed some shreds of national consciousness,

'*If there's an election tomorrow, which general would you vote for?*'

**16. Cartoon, 1966, comments on the army's domination of South Vietnam's
disturbed politics.**

his successors had no nationalist credentials whatsoever. With one exception, every South Vietnamese officer above the rank of lieutenant-colonel (in 1967) had served with the French army against the Vietminh nationalists.[38] Khanh, expelled from the Vietminh for 'tiredness' and lack of discipline, eventually became an officer in the élite gardes mobiles. Ky joined the French when he came of age and trained in France as a bomber pilot. Thieu served against the Vietminh for the duration of the first Indochina War. As Fitzgerald observes, they did not see the war as a national political struggle but 'as an unlooked-for boost to their otherwise unpromising careers'.[39]

Under the Americans they entered into their tawdry inheritance. They were part of the gimcrack élite that enriched itself through contact with the new imperial power. Together with the hotel owners, the licensed importers, the real-estate dealers and the brothel-keepers, they were the people who profited from the war.[40] Thus they were not concerned about the damage that was done to the economy by the huge American military presence. With their connections they need not worry that, by a conservative estimate, the cost of living in the cities rose by 170 per cent between January 1965 and the end of 1967 and that the price of rice, the staple diet, increased 200 per cent. Insouciantly they encouraged the debasement of Vietnamese society, such as an American journalist observed in 1966: 'A drive through Saigon demonstrates another fashion in which the social system works. Virtually all the new construction consists of luxury appartments and office buildings financed by Chinese business-men of affluent Vietnamese with relations or connexions with the régime. The buildings are destined to be rented to Americans. Saigon's workers live, as they always have, in fetid slums on the city's outskirts . . . Bars and bordellos, thousands of young Vietnamese women degrading themselves as bar girls and prostitutes, gangs of hoodlums and beggars and children selling their older sisters and picking pockets have become ubiquitous features of urban life.'[41]

A leadership which actively co-operated with a foreign power whose presence not only corrupted the cities but was also destroying the very fabric of life in the countryside was hardly likely to be popular. With US support and by strong-arm methods the generals held firmly to the fruits of office. While they did so the NLF emerged as the only widely based, though illegal, political movement in South Vietnam. We have seen that, under Diem, the NLF had organized an effective opposition to his regime. In the chaotic situation following his death the NLF strengthened its hold on the countryside. By 1965 it was poised to seize power – hence the massive American intervention. Within five years of being set-up the NLF had created 'a government and an army out of the disordered and intractable society of South Vietnam'.[42] The Front succeeded because it filled the gap created by Saigon regimes whose interests were at odds with the needs of the people and because it was superbly organized.

Responsibility for ensuring 'correct' attitudes and efficient organization was in the hands of cadres drawn from the People's Revolutionary Party. Founded in 1962, it was the Communist Party of South Vietnam and formed the inner core of the NLF. According to one of its own directives it was like a plant and the people were the soil that nourished it.[43] The cadres, after living with the peasants, gradually reorganized the patterns of their daily lives. As they developed personal ties with the villagers they encouraged them to establish village organizations. The most important were the Farmers Associations which decided land disputes, assessed taxes on rice crops, planned irrigation works and organized the defences of the village. Other associations regulated the work of the women and the youth. Everyone participated in village defence through membership of the militia and, in many villages, by making uniforms, weapons and medicines. Given sufficient time, the cadres stimulated the peasants to turn their villages into agricultural co-operatives and military bases. An established Front village might also provide a school, its own newspaper and dispensary and would, in addition, be a training camp for new revolutionaries.

Such remarkable changes were the result of the centralized direction of the PRP, together with the dedication and patience of the cadres. Their patient approach to the peasants contrasted with the generally arrogant and peremptory behaviour of the government officials. One explanation of that contrast is that while the government forces derived their strength from American largesse, the Front depended for its existence on the support of the peasantry. The cadres made a point of stressing their dependence which in fact encouraged the villagers to give their assistance. For many peasants it was a novel and pleasant experience to feel that others depended on them. Such an attitude contributed to a sense of community and allowed the individual villagers to feel that their efforts did have real significance. Commentators on the Front have often undervalued the popular and voluntary element in its organizational success. The Front certainly used strong-arm tactics and in cold-blood killed government officials to strengthen its own position. Generally, however, it succeeded through persuasion rather than by naked violence.

The thoroughness of the NLF was shown in the training it gave its troops. Cadres began by ensuring that the recruits had the right attitude. They destroyed, for example, the political passivity characteristic of so many peasants by inculcating hatred of the enemy. They appreciated that hatred was 'the key to the vast, secret torrents of energy that lay buried within the Vietnamese people...'[44] Only when they had learned to discipline that hatred, to use it 'creatively' were the recruits entrusted with weapons. Politics was paramount. Military training was, however, painstakingly thorough. Attacks on an enemy position might be rehearsed over and over again before the real thing. Morale was kept high by ensuring, for example, that every soldier knew precisely what his role was and why it was important. Self-criticism meetings ensured that mistakes were corrected and also kept lines of communication in the army open to a remarkable degree.

The political and military achievements of the NLF at first owed little to their friends in North Vietnam. From 1959 onwards, it is true, many volunteers, mostly of southern origin, infiltrated south to join the Front. In addition the North Vietnamese provided some armaments by way of the Ho Chi Minh trail. However, Northern participation in the war was marginal until the very success of the largely independent NLF forces precipitated the US bombing of North Vietnam.[45] Thereafter the North Vietnamese became increasingly involved. Despite the US bombing the Hanoi government was able to send support to the NLF and to reinforce them with their own troops. When the Americans launched their offensive there were only some 400 North Vietnamese regulars in the south. By December 1965 there were 14,000; at the end of 1967 the number was 55,000. The bulk of the fighting in the south was still being done by the various groups under the NLF – some 240,000 of them.[46] More and more, however, the southerners were dependent on the North. Meanwhile the North was being obliged to wage its own war against the US Air Force.

The American leaders maintained, as usual, that they were bombing military targets only in the North. However, eye-witness reports of damage to non-military targets, such as hospitals, and accounts of civilian casualties were so numerous and from such reliable sources that the official version was quickly discredited.[47] Even according to a CIA estimate, by 1966, after 161,000 tons of bombs had fallen, there had been almost 30,000 civilian casualties.[48] While the casualties continued to mount, they did not have the effect desired by the Johnson administration. In October 1966 McNamara informed the President that popular morale in the

17. One-man air-raid shelters in Hanoi.

North had not been significantly weakened by the air strikes. He noted, furthermore, that North Vietnam had been able to improvise transportation and that, 'because of the primitive nature of their economy', Rolling Thunder would affect only a small fraction of the people. There was 'very little hope' that Ho Chi Minh would lose control of the population. Confident of popular support, the government was vigorously prosecuting the war. McNamara's memorandum pointed out that, despite difficulties created by the bombs, the communists had actually increased the southward flow of supplies and manpower. Hanoi's determination to support the 'insurgency' was as firm as ever.[49]

Neither Johnson nor the Joint Chiefs were convinced by McNamara's argument in favour of 'stabilizing' Rolling Thunder. The pressure on the North was maintained and then increased. The so-called 'pauses' in the bombing were public relations exercises, intended to deceive the American public, not in fact to de-escalate. In 1967 US planes mined rivers in the North and bombed industrial targets near Hanoi. During the same year the air-war in Laos was also secretly intensified.[50] Still it remained ineffectual. McConnell, Air Force Chief of Staff, was moved to complain that he had 'never been so goddam frustrated'. Morale in North Vietnam, despite the terrible destruction, maiming and loss of life remained high.

The whole nation had been mobilized for the war effort. Children and older people were evacuated from the more obvious targets. Those who remained re-arranged their daily lives. Movement of supplies, for example, took place at night when targets were more difficult to identify. Important materials were dispersed to make them harder to hit. Ingenious means were devised for repairing quickly the roads, railways and bridges that were repeatedly bombed and promptly made viable again. As much as possible was carried on bicycles – a primitive but effective and almost invulnerable form of transport. Armed with MIG fighters and Soviet SAM, surface-to-air missiles, the defence forces accounted for some 1,400 US aircraft between 1965 and 1968.

Together the NLF and the North Vietnamese refused to yield even after enduring a bloody mauling from the world's greatest military power. After three terrible years it was not they who cracked but Lyndon Johnson. The war ended his career and had also the most profound effect on the whole of the United States.

Eight

THE EFFECT OF THE WAR ON
THE UNITED STATES

During the period between the two Presidential elections of 1964 and 1968 the war in Vietnam became the major issue in the political life of the United States. Few people in 1964 could have imagined that, within four years, the war would deny Johnson the chance of re-election. The voters who thought they had given a landslide victory to the peace candidate naturally expected US involvement to remain at a low level. Johnson was, however, as we have seen, preparing to deepen that involvement. Appreciating the lack of enthusiasm in Congress and among the public for such a move, he escalated the war by stealth. In doing so he assumed that America's military might would soon defeat the NLF and its allies from North Vietnam, which he once contemptuously dismissed as a 'raggedy-ass little fourth-rate country'.[1] There would be protests from those he regarded as 'extreme' liberals but he expected that most Americans would quickly accept a *fait accompli*. South Vietnam would be secure and in the USA Johnson would, through a programme of social reform, create the Great Society.

One of his reasons for taking a hard line on the war was to protect himself against right-wingers who might oppose his reform legislation. 'If I don't go in now,' he said, 'and they show later I should have gone, then they'll be all over me in Congress. They won't be talking about my civil rights bill, or education or beautification [of the environment]. No sir, they'll push Vietnam up my ass every time. Vietnam. Vietnam. Vietnam. Right up my ass.'[2] Having 'gone in' his right flank, so to speak, was secure. Since the intervention would be over quickly, the left-wing opposition would, he calculated, soon fizzle out.

The 'success' of another military venture in April 1965 suggested that a show of force in Vietnam might be equally effective. Claiming that a revolution, which in fact was attempting to remove an unpopular dictator, was a communist plot, Johnson despatched 23,000 US marines to the Dominican Republic. The revolution was quickly crushed and American interests preserved. Critics complained about his high-handed action but he ignored them and the incident made little impact on the mass of the people. Johnson's intention was to dispose of the Vietnam problem in the same uncompromising way.[3]

There was a certain plausibility about his approach. Americans had in the past accepted an intemperate use of force by their governments, with only a minority, as in the Dominican affair, affected by scruples of conscience. Furthermore, the disparity in resources between the US and its opponents was likely to ensure rapid results. Such calculations, however, did not take account of the enemy's tenacity. Under the most concentrated assault the Vietnamese remained defiant. As the war dragged on the US victory stayed elusive, opposition to it grew. By prolonging the conflict the Vietnamese forced the American people to consider what it was doing to their own society and to ask what kind of society it was that could get involved in such a war. During the whole of the Cold War period conformity had been an American virtue. Loyalty oaths, congressional investigations, emphasis on the state ideology in schools, manipulation of public opinion by the media – all had conditioned Americans to feel that the questioning of their institutions was unpatriotic. The Vietnam War, however, was called into question, particularly by young Americans. Once the questioning began it did not stop at the war which, after all, was only a product of the society as a whole.

Charles Reich in *The Greening of America* commented that: '. . . the war seemed to sum up the evils of our society: destruction of people, destruction of environment, depersonalized use of technology, war by the rich and powerful against the poor and helpless, justification based on abstract rationality, hypocrisy and lies, and a demand that the individual, regardless of his conscience, values or self, make himself into a part of the war machine, an impersonal projectile bringing death to other people.'[4] Only a minority of Americans were moved to such radical criticism. However, in a country so populous as the United States even a minority could be substantial and included among the critics were men of some influence. Senator Fulbright, for example, chairman of the Senate Foreign Relations Committee, was, like Reich,

18. **Young Americans in an anti-war protest.**

critical of the power in the USA of the military-industrial complex.

In his Farewell Address to the Nation in 1961 President Eisenhower had sounded a warning to his fellow Americans. 'In the councils of Government,' he said, 'we must guard against the acquisition of unwarranted influence . . . by the military-industrial complex. The potential for the disastrous rise of misplaced power exists and will persist. We must never let the weight of this combination endanger our liberties or democratic processes.'[5] His warning went largely unheeded. Nearly seven years later Fulbright pointed out that a large sector of the economy was dependent on so-called 'defence' expenditure. The industries and businesses supplying military needs were, he said, the largest producers of

97

goods and services in the United States. During the fiscal year 1968–9 they would 'pour some $45 billion into over 5,000 cities and towns where over 8 million Americans, counting members of the Armed Forces . . . approximately 10 percent of the labor force, would earn their living from defense spending'.[6] The generals, industrialists and businessmen who manipulated such vast expenditures inevitably constituted a major political force. Together with the politicians, workers, writers and advertising men involved with them, they were a powerful group concerned to perpetuate foreign military commitments, to introduce and expand new weapons systems and so ensure, in Fulbright's words, 'the militarization of large segments of our national life'.[7] Unlike other groups, the military-industrial complex was so enormous that there was no effective counterweight to it.

The longer the Vietnam War lasted the more people began to appreciate just how powerful it had become and to realize the consequences of having so much power concentrated in such hands. The war did not create the military-industrial complex; it did, however, emphasize its influence and prompted its critics to speak out – even if rather belatedly. An editorial in the *New York Times* of 1 September 1967, for example, voiced its concern about the power of the Pentagon. It claimed that the inability of the Congress to uncover the truth (by then widely suspected) about the Tonkin Gulf incident had 'underscored the erosion in the constitutional requirement for legislative control over the war making power'.[8] There no longer existed in fact the constitutional balance that, in theory, kept the military power under civilian control.

The Times was commenting publicly on a state of affairs that was well known to insiders in the political world – that there was a division of opinion between the Secretary of Defense, McNamara, and the military hierarchy. By the autumn of 1967 McNamara was sceptical about military victory. Nevertheless the generals continued to argue that if they were given the tools – specifically more troops – they could finish the job. In such a situation only the President had the authority to 'restore civilian control of national policy'. At that juncture, however, he was desperately hoping that the war was still winnable. He felt that McNamara had 'gone dovish' on him and in November decided to remove him from office.[9] His removal did nothing to allay criticism from other quarters. Senator Thurston Morton of Kentucky, for example, attacked Johnson for allowing himself to be brainwashed by the military-industrial complex into believing that there could still be a military solution in Vietnam.[10]

Congressmen had good reason to feel that their own power had been usurped. The most glaring example of that usurpation was that the war was being fought without the constitutional requirements being fulfilled. According to the Constitution, Congress alone has the power to declare war. It had not, however, legitimized hostilities against North Vietnam, although the executive had chosen to regard the Tonkin Gulf resolution as a functional declaration of war.[11] When we reflect on how that resolution was passed it is clear (and was by 1967 obvious to many Congressmen) that the elected representatives of the people had been manipulated by the President and his advisers. The fact that Americans were killing and being killed in an undeclared war indicated that the constitutional processes had lost some of their validity.[12] It was all the more ominous that, while more and more representatives were objecting to the situation, many were prepared to accept it. Congress continued to vote the money necessary to pursue policies which were in large measure determined by the Pentagon. Congressmen were ready to condemn critics of the war for their 'sense of utter irresponsibility' while they themselves allowed the executive and the military establishment to go beyond their legal authority. Although many were roused to protest against the conduct of the war, the majority were willing to rubber-stamp decisions made by unelected, unrepresentative élites.[13] However, as the results of those decisions became known the dissentient voices increased inside and outside the Congress.

Perhaps the most tragic consequence for Americans were the war casualties. Despite the strategy of replacing manpower with firepower and despite a highly efficient provision of medical services in the combat zones, US casualties multiplied as the war continued. Less than 2,000 Americans were killed in Vietnam in 1965. In 1966 the figure was 5,000 and in 1968 it was 14,000. By the end of 1967 the dead and wounded exceeded 100,000.[14] As the coffins and the maimed veterans returned home many people who had loyally waved the flag began to wonder whether President Thieu and his regime were after all worth such sacrifices.

Though significant, the casualty figures directly affected a small percentage of the total population. On the other hand, the material, as opposed to the human, cost of the war affected all Americans in some measure. With full-scale US intervention in Vietnam there had been a dramatic increase, from $105 million to more than $2,000 million per month.[15] Characteristically, the Johnson administration attempted to conceal the true cost, claiming that it was some $800 million per month. To admit the true figure might, Johnson felt, threaten his Great Society legislation. While Congress might be persuaded to finance either an expensive war or the social reforms he desired, it was unlikely to underwrite both. The President did not doubt that the reforms would be sacrificed first. He therefore lied about the military expenditure. The Council of Economic Advisers, increasingly sceptical about the government's statistics, demanded more exact estimates and urged a tax increase to meet some of the cost. Fearing that it might give the game away, Johnson delayed his request for an increase in taxes and so helped to create an inflation whose political impact became 'almost as serious a political issue in 1968 as the war itself'.[16] The President eventually suggested an income tax surcharge in his budget message of January 1967 – a proposal which was not agreed by Congress until the summer of 1968, by which time the inflation was 'full-blown' and was provoking a great deal of anti-war sentiment.

The sheer scale of expenditure (which could not be concealed for ever) also created doubts. Was it possible, even with the enormous resources of the USA, to devote nearly $30,000 million every year to the Vietnam War? Was it necessary to spend so much to defeat a nation of backward peasants? Senator Hartke threw some light on that question in a magazine article about a huge amphibious operation in the Mekong Delta, to which US taxpayers contributed $16 million. Since a total of 21 Vietcong were killed, the cost of a single enemy death was no less than $800,000.[17] Another senator commented on the anomaly of spending $66 million per day 'trying to save the 16 million people of South Vietnam while leaving the plight of 20 million urban poor [in the USA] unresolved'.[18] (The South Vietnamese might have doubted whether the bombs, napalm and so on paid for by the $66 million were indeed intended to 'save' them.) A similar point was made by a prominent retired general, Gavin, who early in 1967 recommended, in testimony before the Senate Foreign

Relations Committee, ending the conflict as quickly and as reasonably as possible. He later remarked that America's domestic programmes were 'grossly underfunded, especially in the poverty area . . . as a consequence of the Vietnam war'.[19]

Such criticisms helped to intensify opposition to the war, particularly when riots by black Americans in 1965 and 1967 seemed to confirm the thesis that the enormous cost of the war was inhibiting much needed social reform. That specific point demands some further consideration. While the Vietnamese imbroglio undoubtedly had an important impact on the racial question, its effect was not to be measured simply in terms of finance.

President Johnson had made a brave attempt to tackle the racial issue, perhaps the most intractable of America's social problems. The passing of the Civil Rights Act of 1964 and the Voting Rights Act of 1965 sought to fulfil some of the promises made to black Americans a hundred years previously. It was soon clear, however, that they were by no means satisfied by such belated guarantees of their rights as citizens. In August 1965, the very month in which the Voting Rights Act was passed, they rioted for a week in Los Angeles. Thirty-four people died, over a thousand were injured and some six hundred buildings were destroyed or seriously damaged. Two years later there were even more serious disturbances in over sixty cities across the United States, particularly in Newark and Detroit. In July 1967, more than a thousand black militants from all over America attended a Black Power conference. Their leaders asserted their right to control their own destiny, demanding not extra handouts from the Federal Government but an end to the exploitative system that had kept them a subject race. They condemned the war in Vietnam not simply because it diverted dollars away from the black ghettos but because it was a foreign parallel to the subjection of the blacks in the USA. They compared themselves with the Vietnamese: both were, in their view, victims of a racist white government, prepared to use violence to protect its power at home and abroad.

That point had been made in 1965 by a former president of Students for a Democratic Society who alleged that the murders in Vietnam were similar to the murders of blacks in the American South. The refusal to deal with the needs and aspirations of people in Vietnam was, he said, the same as the refusal to deal with the problems of millions of poor people in the USA. What kind of system was it, he enquired, that allowed the US or any other country to 'seize the destinies of other people and use them callously for their own ends'?[20] Both militant black Americans and radical young white Americans attacked 'the system' in the USA. The manifesto of a conference attended by both groups in 1967 declared that whoever was running America, it was not the American people. Delegates went on to promise an end to the devastation of Vietnam and the destruction of other countries by the 'economic and political pressures of the great powers . . .'[21] In the event, advocates of Black Power were unwilling to co-operate with the whites and the two movements went their separate ways. Both, however, remained united in their condemnation of the Vietnam War, the most outrageous product of a system which they both reviled.

Radical young Americans discovered a number of ways to express their opposition to the war and the system. They campaigned against conscription by publicly burning their draft cards and refusing to be inducted into the armed services. They attacked the system of selective service which, by deferring military service for those who had gained certain academic qualifications, ensured that many more of the poor than of the middle and upper-income groups were called up. Files in draft centres were destroyed and some of those who were academically qualified refused to take the tests which could have guaranteed them deferment. Troop trains were delayed by people sitting on the railway lines. Other forms of sit-ins were held in university campuses. Teach-ins were also organized to counteract the official version of the war. Underground newspapers were published and underground organizations emerged to help draft resisters to avoid jail by fleeing abroad. Mass demonstrations were held at which the resisters came into violent conflict with the police and national guardsmen.

In October 1967 tens of thousands of mainly young people participated in a mass peace demonstration in Washington, culminating in a march on the Pentagon building. Johnson subsequently praised the soldiers and police for their outstanding performance in containing 'violence and lawlessness'.[22] His opinion echoed those of millions of Americans who considered the opponents of the war as no better than traitors. Even so the active critics did prevent the powerful state propaganda apparatus from going unchallenged; their campaigns did make some impact on the government and on other Americans whose critical faculties were not totally blunted by an excess of patriotism. One of the prominent national figures who demonstrated at the Pentagon, Noam Chomsky, later commented on the various anti-war activities: 'Resistance cannot now significantly deplete the manpower pool that makes possible the use of American power for global repression, nor can it, at the moment, significantly impede the research, production and supply on which this exercise of power rests. But it can contribute significantly towards raising the domestic costs of this attempt and eliminating the apathy and passivity that may permit it to succeed.'[23]

While the main opponents of the war were the young, there was much criticism also from some of the intellectuals. Such critics were not a homogeneous group. There were two broad categories of protest which have been described as 'responsible' and 'hysterical'. The 'responsible' protests came from those who did not make sweeping denunciations of the American system. They opposed the war on the purely pragmatic grounds that the cost of winning it was proving unacceptable. Arthur Schlesinger, the historian, typified that attitude. In his book *The Bitter Heritage* he questioned the conduct of the war and showed concern about its consequences in the United States, fearing, for example, that some of the war's more extreme critics might, as a result of the backlash against them, be 'preparing the way for a new McCarthyism'.[24] Schlesinger was doubtful about the judgment of a right-wing journalist that the war might, after all, be winnable. In his next sentence, however, he commented: 'We all pray that Mr. Alsop will be right.'[25] Clearly, Schlesinger had no doubt that the US was entitled to intervene in the internal affairs of Vietnam. He recognized that intervention had led to the imposition in the South of a 'régime pervaded by nepotism, corruption and cynicism'.[26] Furthermore, he admitted that, if Americans continued to pursue military victory, they would leave 'the tragic country gutted and devastated by bombs, burned by napalm, turned into a wasteland by chemical defoliation, a land of ruin and wrack'.[27] Nevertheless, he did not favour an American withdrawal from Vietnam. Instead, he recommended a more discriminating use of military power in order to 'hold the line' in the South. He still believed that the United States was entitled to use force to achieve its objective of a South Vietnamese bastion against 'international communism'.

The more extreme or 'hysterical' critics of the war denied the right of Americans to be in Vietnam at all. 'The proper question,' said one, 'is not whether the United States can win at an acceptable cost, but whether it should be involved at all in the internal affairs of Indochina.'[28] Their answer was that it should not. They appreciated, however, that the Vietnamese intervention fitted into the pattern of US policy as they perceived it. That policy, like the policy of any major power, was, in their view, determined by the 'national interest'. What constituted that interest was decided by the dominant social groups. The primary aim of those élite groups was to maximize the free access of US capital to 'the markets and human and material resources of the world' and to maintain 'its freedom of operation in a global economy'.[29] Those were the realities behind spurious claims that the Americans were acting to preserve freedom and democracy in South Vietnam. Predictably, given such a view of American motives, the radical critics were very outspoken about the intervention itself. Chomsky, for example, considered that US policy in Vietnam was no more debatable than the rape of Abyssinia by Mussolini or the Soviet intervention in Hungary in 1956. 'The war,' he said, 'is simply an obscenity, a depraved act by weak and miserable men, including all of us, who have allowed it to go on and on with endless fury and destruction – all of us who would have remained silent had stability and order been secured.'[30]

Chomsky's views were more forceful than they were representative. There were, indeed, many intellectuals who considered that even Schlesinger's much less radical strictures were unacceptable. Almost any aspersions against the generals were unwelcome to those who had made a niche in the military-industrial complex. Senator Fulbright pointed out that, since professors, no less than businessmen, liked money and influence, they were eager to accept contracts offered by the military establishment. Naturally, there were no contracts for critics and those who signed on also signed away their freedom to question the government's policies. Many in fact were prepared to be agents rather than critics of those policies: too often academic honesty was 'no less marketable than a box of detergent on the grocery shelf'.[31]

Their attitudes were shared by millions of workers, businessmen, bankers, technicians and so on who were also prospering as a result of the war economy.[32] Even in 1967 when victory still seemed elusive, public opinion remained hawkish. Harris Survey polls in February, July and August all showed that over 70 per cent of Americans supported the war. In September the figure fell to 58 per cent, but rose again to 61 per cent in December.[33] In that month delegates to the annual convention of the AFL-CIO re-affirmed overwhelmingly their support for Johnson's Vietnam policy.[34]

Johnson was aware, however, that there was widespread discontent, even if a sense of patriotism dissuaded many ordinary people from disowning their President publicly in the middle of a war. Reacting privately to the substantial number who did in fact criticize him, he complained: 'The only difference between the Kennedy assassination and mine is that I am alive and it has been more tortuous.'[35] In public, he persisted in maintaining that the enemy was 'hurting' and that victory would not be long in coming. While many Americans were prepared, like the President, to be optimistic in public, many others realized that they were being fooled. The credibility gap between the government and the governed continued to grow wider.

As the next Presidential election drew nearer there seemed little chance that Johnson could repeat the triumph he had relished four years previously. Too many things were going wrong. The President had started to build a Great Society but had been diverted from that work by the demands of the war. Such reforms as were achieved were insufficient to prevent black riots on an unprecedented scale. Millions of television sets had shown the blazing buildings of Watts and Newark. They had also shown the anti-war riots. Most important, they had taken the war itself into American homes. It may be that what the Americans did not see was more important than some of the horrors they did see. They did not see the enemy being decisively beaten, while their government claimed that victory was imminent. They saw nothing in fact to reduce the credibility gap. What they did observe was violence begetting violence, both at home and abroad. After the 1964 election Johnson might reasonably have claimed that he was at the head of an unparalleled national consensus embracing labour, the blacks, the middle class and even most of the rich. Long before 1968 that consensus was shattered. Even more seriously for

Johnson's election prospects, he had allowed the Democratic Party to disintegrate. At the beginning of 1968 the *coup de grâce* was delivered to his hopes of re-election by the Tet offensive.

For the first time, the American public saw vividly the toughness of the guerrillas not in remote jungles but in the familiar terrain of a city. 'The pictures of corpses in the garden of the American embassy cut through the haze of argument and counterargument, giving flat contradiction to the official optimism about the slow but steady progress of the war.'[36] LBJ's credibility was blown away entirely by the Vietcong mortars in Saigon. A week after the offensive began, the journalist Art Buchwald gave the quietus to years of military dissembling in a column with the by-line 'Little Big Horn, Dakota: Gen. George Armstrong Custer said today in an exclusive interview with this correspondent that the battle of the Little Big Horn had just turned the corner and he could now see the light at the end of the tunnel. "We have the Sioux on the run", Gen. Custer told me.'[37]

By the end of March it was clear to Johnson that the prospect of his re-election was fading fast. Results of primary elections showed that the public had turned against him. As we have seen, he directed the bombing campaign away from the North and at the same time withdrew from the race for the presidency. The election campaign was eventually fought for the Democrats by Hubert Humphrey who had become prominent as a reformer but had later compromised his liberal support by a total adherence, when he was Vice-President, to Johnson's Vietnam policy. The Republican candidate was Richard Nixon, Vice-President under Eisenhower and Kennedy's rival for the presidency in 1960. His career had been built on his record as an uncompromising anticommunist and in 1968 he emphasized his opposition to radicalism with a strong commitment to 'law and order'. On Vietnam he was cagey. Feeling that Humphrey, with the albatross of LBJ's policy around his neck, was a marked man, he himself wanted to create as few vibrations as possible on that issue. His tactics seemed to be succeeding when in September the polls showed him leading Humphrey by 45 to 30 points.

Very late in the campaign, Humphrey began to disassociate himself from Johnson's stance on the war. His new posture and Nixon's continuing refusal to commit himself reduced the gap between the two men. Eventually Nixon won the election by the narrow margin of 500,000 votes in a total poll of 63 million, having by his hesitancy turned a potential landslide into a cliffhanger.[38] Both Nixon and Humphrey were party stalwarts, unlikely to make any fundamental change in America's relations with Vietnam. One candidate who might possibly have been more responsive to the public mood, Robert Kennedy, was murdered in the course of the campaign.

Nine

NIXON'S CONTINUING PURSUIT OF VICTORY

Nixon came to power pledged to 'end the war and win the peace'. His method of winning the peace was to continue direct American involvement in the war until January 1973. During the first three years of his presidency 15,000 Americans were killed in Vietnam.[1] In the first two years the US Air Force dropped 2,539,743 million tons of bombs in Indochina – more than the total tonnage expended by America during the Second World War.[2] Within two days of taking office, Nixon ordered an incursion into Laos by a battalion of marines. (Even Johnson had refrained from a ground attack there.) The new President was, it appeared, not so much a peacemaker as a pacemaker. An American journalist noted later: 'What President Nixon means by peace is what other people mean by victory.'[3]

Johnson's experience persuaded Nixon that he must reduce the number of US ground forces in Indochina. Nevertheless he was confident that victory could be achieved; the objectives remained the same, only the means were to be modified. Thus Nixon adopted a tactic, devised first by Clifford,[4] of withdrawing American combat troops and replacing them with an expanded South Vietnamese army. 'Vietnamization' satisfied both the 'doves' who welcomed the limited US withdrawal and the 'hawks' who wished the war to continue. The American troops having failed to deliver victory, the 'Asian boys' were recruited to do their own fighting, with assistance from US technology. The new policy promised a way of defeating the enemy while keeping American casualties at an acceptable level.

A mobilization law allowed Thieu to call up all men from eighteen to thirty-eight into military service and to form self-defence units from seventeen-year-olds and men from thirty-nine to forty-three.[5] By the end of 1970 he had over a million men under his command. Moreover his troops were equipped by the

Americans with the most up-to-date automatic rifles, grenade-launchers, artillery and other weapons. They were also provided with massive air support from the US Air Force, while the South Vietnamese Air Force was also increased and a growing number of pilots trained in the USA.[6] While the effectiveness of the government forces apparently increased, the NLF had been weakened by losses sustained in 1968 and in the following year. Adams, Westmoreland's successor, carried out an Accelerated Pacification Campaign, as a result of which the Mekong Delta

19. **American marines returning home 1969.**

was seemingly cleared of the Vietcong.[7] The casualties inflicted and the devastation caused by the Ninth Division in the Delta were paralleled by the activities of the Koreans, Marines and the American Division (of My Lai fame) in large areas of central Vietnam. In the light of those events, an American officer engaged in the Vietnamization programme claimed, in October 1969, that the South Vietnamese had been given enough training and equipment to enable them to win the war.[8]

Such optimism was in fact ill-founded. The strengthening of the army merely consolidated the clique that commanded it. In 1965

George Ball, one of the few realists in Johnson's entourage, described South Vietnam as an army without a country. With Nixon's help, the army had become more effective in a military sense but remained politically isolated: it still had no country. Vietnamization simply perpetuated a situation whereby a group of Vietnamese in uniform dominated the rest of the people. It did not create a viable political alternative to the NLF.

Recognizing the political vulnerability of his ally, Nixon intensified a campaign, known as the Phoenix Programme, to destroy the infrastructure of the National Liberation Front. Instituted under American prompting and guidance in 1967, the programme was aimed at rooting out all NLF sympathizers and agents in South Vietnam. With remarkable effrontery the military dictatorship claimed that the Front's infrastructure had, by its fifth-column activities, sabotaged the country's political development. Accordingly, American and South Vietnamese security organizations co-operated to 'neutralize' the undercover Vietcong. In practice many people were liquidated who had no connection with the NLF. One intelligence officer in the US Army who was attached to the Phoenix Programme commented: 'When I arrived in the district I was given a list of 200 names of people who had to be killed. When I left after six months, we still hadn't killed anyone on the list. But we'd killed 260 other people . . .'[9] Many victims were denounced on trumped-up charges; it was an excellent opportunity for the settling of old scores. While ostensibly purging the communists, the security forces were licensed to arrest, torture and kill anyone who opposed the regime. According to the government's own figures, between 1968 and 1971, 81,039 people were convicted, some of whom 'rallied', that is, were persuaded to go over to the government side; 40,994 were killed.[10]

In March 1971 the programme was expanded at a cost to the US government of $1 billion.[11] However, despite such an enormous expenditure of money, not to mention the cost in human life, the campaign failed to destroy the NLF's basis of support. It alienated even more people than were killed and made the regime even less attractive to the ordinary citizens of South Vietnam. While the government had little success against the Front, the NLF did successfully infiltrate the regime. The CIA reported in October 1970 that within the Saigon government there were some thirty thousand people who were prepared to co-operate with the Front, and that their number might soon be fifty thousand.[12]

Despite such unpromising support, Nixon was determined to defeat the North Vietnamese, if necessary by extending the war. Thus in April 1970 he announced the US invasion of Cambodia. He claimed that his action (a 'step towards peace') was forced on him by the NVA and the NLF who were using Cambodia as a sanctuary and were a threat to its independence. It was necessary, he stated, to deny them that refuge in order to win the war in Vietnam. There was little substance in his claim. Although the NLF and their allies had crossed the border to avoid the intensive bombardment of South Vietnam, they were not attempting to seize Cambodia for their own purposes, nor were they using it as a springboard for their war in Vietnam. The border area did not indeed even offer them a very secure retreat. One eyewitness commented early in 1970 that 'there seemed no place the Vietcong could hide, let alone establish a permanent sanctuary'.[13]

In fact, what provoked American intervention in Cambodia was not so much the belligerence of the Vietcong as the neutralism of the Cambodian Head of State, Prince Sihanouk. He pointed out that for years the Americans had been pressing him to fight the NLF and that his refusal had been a major bone of contention between Phnom Penh and Washington.[14] As a result of their interference Sihanouk severed diplomatic relations in 1965. In June 1969 they were resumed in exchange for an American pledge to respect Cambodia's independence and sovereignty. Nevertheless, as a congressional committee later revealed, between March 1969 and May 1970 the Nixon administration waged a secret war against Cambodia. During that period 3,630 B-52 bombing sorties were flown over the country, their activities being concealed from Congress and the public by faking reports, burning order papers and producing false statistics.[15]

On 18 March 1970 Sihanouk was deposed while he was on a visit to Europe. Evidence presented in his book *My War with the CIA* revealed that the US Central Intelligence Agency had paved the way for his deposition. Sihanouk commented that, while the leaders of the plot, Lon Nol and Sirik Matak may have been too stupid to foresee its consequences, the United States 'consciously and deliberately, exported the war in South Vietnam to Cambodia'.[16] On

29 April South Vietnamese forces invaded Cambodia and were joined on 1 May by the Americans. The invaders provided some support for the Lon Nol regime which was under attack from pro-Sihanouk groups. They also destroyed supplies and equipment belonging to the North Vietnamese Army. Little else was achieved before increasing pressure from within the United States forced the withdrawal in July of the American troops.

In the United States the Cambodian invasion had caused widespread protests, the most tragic being at Kent State University where on 4 May Ohio National Guardsmen killed four student demonstrators. Even Congress, usually a toothless watchdog, was provoked into action. In December 1970 both Houses prohibited the introduction of US combat troops or military advisers into Cambodia. The bombing however was to continue until August 1973 when Congress finally forced Nixon to ground the bombers. In the intervening years they devastated much of the country. Even the soil itself was destroyed by a combination of bombs, napalm and chemicals. Such systematic destruction of all living things by saturation bombing caused great bitterness. Sihanouk even compared the American leadership with the Nazis. He asked '. . . what is the difference between burning and gassing people in ovens and doing it to a whole nation out in the open?

" HE TOOK THE WRAPS OFF OUR SECRET WEAPON! "

20.

That is just what the United States of President Nixon is doing today . . . Nixon is waging a war of extermination against the entire people of Indo-China.'[17]

Despite the meagre successes of his ground forces in Cambodia, and in defiance of the protests they had provoked, Nixon authorized an incursion into Laos in February 1971 by 22,000 South Vietnamese troops. Their campaign lasted a mere forty-five days and resulted in heavy casualties for the invaders. A further brief foray in May was equally unsuccessful. Such operations were justified on the grounds that Laos was being protected against invasion from North Vietnam. We might note here that American propaganda paradoxically tended to credit the North Vietnamese with the status of supermen who not only threatened South Vietnam but were also taking over Cambodia and Laos while simultaneously defending themselves against the enormous military might of the United States.[18] It is hardly surprising that convincing evidence of such ubiquitous aggression by North Vietnam was hard to find.

Hanoi did indeed provide support for the Pathet Lao, the indigenous Laotian left-wing forces; the North Vietnamese were determined to do what they could to prevent Laos from becoming a secure American base.[19] They were aware that ever since the creation of the state of Laos the US had been attempting to make it an anti-communist stronghold. From 1946 to 1963 Laos received more US aid per capita than any other country in Southeast Asia.[20] When dollars failed to ensure that Laos was a haven of US influence the American leadership resorted to force. US planes were used to attack the Pathet Lao in 1964[21] and three years later Johnson authorized the bombing of the country by B-52s. To keep their activities hidden every raid over Laos was paralleled by another over South Vietnam. As one commentator remarked, it was 'a form of information control that presumably caused, among other things, some loss of life'.[22] Nixon continued with such clandestine raids, the existence of which was at last officially admitted in 1973 at a hearing of the Senate Armed Services Committee.[23]

In Laos, as in Cambodia, the bombing intensified under Nixon – from some 4,500 sorties a month (before the November 1968 limitation of the campaign against North Vietnam) to between 12,500 and 15,000 sorties a month early in 1970.[24] In April 1970 one correspondent reported that the majority of villages and towns in Northwest Laos had been destroyed. Refugees from the Plain of Jars asserted that they had been bombed almost daily during the previous year and that they had spent most of the previous two years living in caves and holes.[25] Nixon stated in March 1970 that he was concerned about protecting American and South Vietnamese forces who were threatened by the infiltration of North Vietnamese troops and supplies along the Ho Chi Minh trail. It is worth noting that the Laotian section of that trail lay 200 miles south-east of the Plain of Jars. The scale of the bombing, moreover suggests that the US objective was not so much to protect the lives of their troops by blocking the movement of supplies but to destroy as much as possible of Laos and to force the resettlement of the population in order to weaken the revolutionary forces in the country. Although that policy killed many civilians and devastated the land, paradoxically it raised the morale of the guerrillas, making them more determined to oust a government that co-operated with the Americans.[26]

A significant feature of the American activities in Laos, Cambodia and also in Vietnam was the extent to which they were concealed from the public. The concealment practised by the administrations of Truman, Eisenhowever, Kennedy and, in particular, of President Johnson, was exposed dramatically in June 1971 with the publication by the *New York Times* of the 'Pentagon Papers'. Comprising 3,000 pages of narrative history and 4,000 pages of documents, they were a top-secret history of American involvement in Indochina from the Second World War to May 1968. This historical survey was commissioned by Secretary of Defense McNamara in 1967 when he was increasingly concerned about the war and was anxious to discover how the United States had become embroiled. Daniel Ellsberg, one of its authors, having become highly critical of a policy which previously he had supported, illegally delivered copies of most of the material to the *New York Times*. Despite attempts by the Nixon administration to prevent them, *The Times* and the *Washington Post* published the information, their action being later upheld by the Supreme Court. Their revelations about, for example, the handling of the Tonkin Gulf affair, the decision to begin Rolling Thunder, the surreptitious build-up of ground forces from 1965 and so on, have been incorporated into the present account. At the time of their publication they confirmed the suspicions and doubts of the war's critics. In the opinion of the most outspoken opponents of official policy, they 'provided documentary evidence of a conspiracy to use force in international affairs in violation of law'.[27] Even those who were not quite so hostile to the whole tenor of US policy were appalled by the deception practised upon them.[28]

Neil Sheehan, the reporter who was principally responsible for the *New York Times*' presentation of the Pentagon documents, was left with one overriding impression – that the government of the USA was not what he had thought it was. Within the government he discerned a centralized state. For the men who formed that inner government, the enemy was not merely the communists but also their own press, judiciary and Congress. They operated in secret not so much to keep hostile foreign powers in the dark as to escape judgment on their competence by their own population. Each administration avoided exposing the weaknesses of its predecessor: essentially the same people were, after all, running the successive governments. In Sheehan's opinion, such a code of secrecy encouraged underhand actions, supposedly to safeguard 'national security'. While the ordinary citizens could take pride in their democratic institutions, those at the very centre of power would do their dirty work for them. Thus the President might regale the public with disquisitions on peace, freedom and democracy while, with his closest advisers, he spoke the language of realpolitik.[29]

Many Americans were indeed unwilling to recognize some of the dreadful things that were being done, in the name of security, by their leaders. They did not wish to be shown, for example, that 'search and destroy' missions could lead to massacres such as occurred in the village of My Lai.[30] There, on 16 March 1968, American troops deliberately and indiscriminately slaughtered more than five hundred people – men, women and children. The story of the massacre was not made public until November 1969; attempts to reveal the facts previously had been thwarted.[31] When the story was eventually published many Americans refused to believe it. A poll taken in St. Louis showed that only 12 per cent of those who had heard the facts accepted them as true.[32] One reaction to the grisly story was that 'this sort of thing should have been kept classified'.[33]

Many other massacres were kept classified or were given little publicity; My Lai was by no means unique.[34] We have already seen that the American method of waging war in Indochina resulted in the wholesale killing of civilians from the air. It would be surprising to find the ground troops, who were generally at much greater risk, showing more restraint than the bomber pilots. In fact they were encouraged to regard all Vietnamese as inferiors – 'slopes', 'slant-eyes', 'gooks' and 'dinks'. (Significantly, in General Westmoreland's headquarters there were separate toilet facilities for Americans and Vietnamese.[35]) Most US soldiers followed the 'mere gook rule', according to which 'anything that moves and has a yellow skin is an enemy, unless there is incontrovertible evidence to the contrary'.[36] Conditioning them to regard the Vietnamese as sub-humans made it easier for them to kill and commit atrocities.[37] Racist attitudes, we might note, were not exclusive to the ordinary GI. Townsend Hoopes, former Under-Secretary of the Air Force and 'one of the most humane and enlightened voices to be heard within the mainstream of American opinion', commented that '. . . happiness, wealth and power are expectations that constitute a dimension far beyond the experience, and probably beyond the emotional comprehension of the Asian poor'.[38] His assumption that peasants in Asia are incapable of happiness is on a par with a belief common in the West that life is cheap to Asians, that they are cruel and barbaric to their own people and that they do not share civilized Western values. Similar assumptions were made about American Indians: the mass slaughter of the Indians found a parallel in the ruthlessness shown to the Vietnamese.[39] One American commentator was prompted to ask: 'would we have pursued quite such policies – and quite such military tactics – if the Vietnamese were white?'[40]

The tactic of indiscriminate killing was not only a crime but also a blunder. Many Vietnamese, and Laotians and Cambodians, were convinced that the US was launched on a course of genocide. Believing that, they were constrained to fight back, whatever the odds. The simple desire for self-preservation (they did, *pace* Hoopes, care for life) helped to explain the remarkable resilience of the NLF and the North Vietnamese. So resilient were they that by the spring of 1972 they were ready to begin a new major offensive in South Vietnam, where conditions were giving cause for alarm to those with eyes to see. One American correspondent observed: 'It could be as long as two or three years before the

Reds take over. But it could be this summer or as early as Tet.'[41]

The economic situation in South Vietnam had suffered as a result of the withdrawal of American forces and the consequent reduction of the flow of US dollars. Inflation was a major problem and it was expected that by the summer of 1972 the government would start simply printing money to pay its bills.[42] The closure of American bases also added to the considerable number of the unemployed. Furthermore, of the population of 17 million people some 5 million were refugees, many of whom lived in and around the cities and towns. As a result of the widespread destruction of the countryside, South Vietnam was more urbanized than Switzerland.[43] Ex-peasants huddled together in shanty towns, dependent on hand-outs for their survival. Economic grievances were compounded by political repression. Commenting on the condition of his country a Vietnamese doctor pointed out that 'the counter appeal to communism must be material or moral. But on the one hand are rising prices, unemployment. On the other, corruption, no real democracy, above all, no real patriotism.'[44]

The despair of the South Vietnamese was matched by the low morale of the remaining American troops, their discipline undermined by 'radical politics, racial tension and sheer indifference'.[45] Officers and NCOs were chary of exercising their authority for fear of being 'fragged', that is, attacked by their own men with fragmentation grenades. Drug taking among the troops was endemic. Smoking 'pot' was commonplace and in May 1971 the Army Secretary stated that there was between 10 and 15 per cent hard drug addiction in the Vietnam command.[46]

The brunt of the 1972 spring offensive was borne not by the demoralized Americans but by the equally despondent army of South Vietnam. What little enthusiasm they had for the war was shattered by General Giap's 130 mm guns. After the fall of Quang Tri the remaining soldiers of the 3rd. Division and the Rangers went wild with panic and fled, leaving their wounded to die by the roadside.[47] After a disastrous opening phase the South Vietnamese leadership did recover its nerve. Furthermore, the US intensified its bombing campaign: in April Nixon rseumed the bombing of North Vietnam. Giap's offensive did not, as initially seemed likely, sweep all before it. Nevertheless the NLF and the North Vietnamese Army made considerable gains. By October the army of South Vietnam was short of strategic fighting units;

those remaining were unable to recapture the 'liberated' areas. In one month the Vietcong, having drawn away the main units of Thieu's army, had assumed control of the Delta. Divisions of the North Vietnamese Army were massing on the border with Cambodia. The senior American adviser in the Delta considered that the situation was 'back where it was in 1965'.[48]

The enemy's successes were of particular concern to Nixon since the presidential election was due in November. The Watergate affair has revealed how determined he was to be re-elected. In February 1972, for example, his associates forged letters to discredit Senator Muskie, one of the contenders for the nomination of the Democratic Party. Senator McGovern, Nixon's eventual challenger, had long been opposed to the Vietnam War which he promised to end quickly if elected. Nixon sought to undermine McGovern not only by corrupting the electoral process but also by attempting to resolve the issue of the war before the election. His response to the enemy's spring offensive was to bomb Hanoi into submission. Evidently he still believed that victory could be achieved if sufficient force were applied against North Vietnam. His new offensive was even more concentrated than the bombing carried out under Johnson. There were virtually no restrictions on targets: Hanoi and Haiphong were attacked immediately. Nixon even agreed to the mining of North Vietnamese ports, a move Johnson had eschewed because of its possible international repercussions. Littauer, an authority on the air-war, pointed out in May 1972 that the US was dropping 3,000 tons per day on Indochina, at a daily cost of $20 million.[49] The raids on the North quickly negated the enormous effort at reconstruction made there since the end of the 1968 offensive – new port facilities, roads and bridges were some of the targets destroyed. According to the Swedish Chargé d'Affaires in Hanoi, the bombers 'had hit everything worth hitting'.[50] A French eyewitness reported that Nam Dinh, the third largest city in North Vietnam, was four-fifths destroyed. Shops, schools, flats and most of a 300-bed hospital were flattened by raid after raid. In the end it appeared that the US pilots were intent on simply pulverizing the ruins.[51]

Remarkably, morale remained high and the war effort continued. In Nam Dinh, for example, essential services were organized underground or dispersed in the neighbouring countryside. After the destruction of a large textile mill, production continued in ten thatched buildings outside the city.[52] The toughness and ingenuity of the North Vietnamese greatly reduced the military effectiveness of the bombing, although a great price had to be paid in lost lives, injury and material destruction. The bombing did not prevent a good harvest, a point of crucial importance in a land where 90 per cent of the population lived in the countryside.

Given the failure of the air offensive to enforce the capitulation of North Vietnam and bearing in mind the desperate situation in the South, Nixon was constrained to try another tactic before the Americans went to the polls. For years peace talks had dragged on fruitlessly in Paris. In October 1972 the President allowed Kissinger his principal adviser on foreign policy, to negotiate a draft agreement with the North Vietnamese on ending hostilities. Its terms were published shortly before the presidential election and bombing above the 20th parallel was restricted. The public in the United States and indeed throughout the world were led to believe that peace was imminent. McGovern's lack-lustre campaign had already indicated that Nixon would have an easy victory. Kissinger's manoeuvrings in Paris ensured him a landslide, in which he gained a majority in 49 of the 50 states, on 7 November.

The American government had delayed signing the draft agreement before Nixon's re-election. After the victory was won Kissinger was given a new brief which was, in effect, to repudiate the agreement they had previously accepted. Under Point 1 of the draft, the United States had respected the unity of Vietnam as recognized by the 1954 Geneva Agreement. In December, however, Kissinger insisted that Hanoi accept at least implicitly the division of Vietnam and thus the sovereignty of Thieu's government in the South.[53] It would appear that the October negotiations had been occasioned not so much by a genuine concern to end the fighting as by electoral expediency on the part of the Nixon administration. When the North Vietnamese refused to accept the new terms negotiations broke down and Nixon began a further air attack against the North which outdid in intensity even the formidable bombardment of the summer.

During the first week of the new campaign 18,000 tons of bombs were dropped on North Vietnam.[54] Two French journalists in Hanoi, a city of 1 million people, were told that the bombing was killing 200 and wounding 200 of its inhabitants every day. They observed the bombed ruins of Bach Mai hospital, noting wryly the Pentagon claim that no civilian objective in Hanoi had been destroyed by bombs. They stated that the Kham Tien quarter, with 28,000 inhabitants, had been 'ground to nothing by night carpet-bombing'. The B-52s had devastated an area one and half miles long and several hundred yards wide, where most of the houses had been atomized.[55] As information about the damage was published there was widespread criticism in the United States and in many other countries. In Britain, Professor Denis Brogan, one of the foremost authorities on and a life-long friend of the USA, expressed his outrage at a policy which, sustained for a number of years and then renewed with unprecedented violence, appeared 'to be equal to any of the war crimes for which high-ranking German or Japanese officers were executed after the Second World War'.[56]

Nixon's latest turn of the screw was short-lived. Early in January 1973 negotiations were resumed and at the end of the month a ceasefire was agreed by both sides. It has been commonly assumed that, since the renewal of negotiations followed so soon after the Christmas bombing, Nixon's tactics, however repugnant, were at least effective. Several considerations cast doubt on that assumption. First, the morale in the North remained high even at the height of the bombing. An American clergyman wrote from Hanoi at the end of the first week of the latest offensive : 'So life goes on here. The streets still are full of bicycles and the children still smile as we four Americans pass by. But many people are being evacuated. They say everything of any strategic worth has long since gone. There are only the people, and I see no signs of weakening. They say they have fought for independence for 1,000 years and they won't stop now.'[57] One of the reasons for their impressive belligerence was the sudden vulnerability of the B-52s. During the first week of the December raids the North Vietnamese shot down ten, each costing £3,400,000.[58] Their sharpshooting gravely embarrassed the American President. Since coming to power he had used every practicable resource available in his quest for victory. Cambodia and Laos had been invaded, Haiphong harbour had been mined, unrestricted air-war had been waged against all Indochina. For obvious reasons the use of nuclear weapons and a massive re-deployment of US ground troops were ruled out. With characteristic tenacity Nixon had done his utmost to win a war which in 1968 Johnson and many other Americans

had recognized as unwinnable. By 1973 even he was convinced that direct military intervention by the United States should be abandoned.

Obviously the North Vietnamese were relieved when the bombing ended but they had not resumed negotiations simply to obtain that relief. The fact was that the Nixon–Kissinger tactic of the carpet-bombing of urban centres failed. In January they were obliged to accept (although, as we shall see, with the greatest cynicism) an agreement which was virtually identical to the proposals Hanoi had put forward the previous October.[59]

Ten

PEACE AND WAR

The agreements of January 1973 were not expected to resolve all the conflicts in Vietnam; at best, it was felt, they might create a respite during which a solution of sorts could begin to emerge. The situation was in some ways analogous to that of 1954 and the terms of the ceasefire covered some of the issues included in the Geneva Accords.[1] As in 1954, it was agreed that the eventual reunification of Vietnam should be 'carried out step by step through peaceful means'.[2] Accordingly, the 1973 agreement reiterated that the demilitarized zone was not a boundary separating sovereign states but a temporary demarcation line. Again, it was recognized that the South Vietnamese people as a whole should decide the political future of South Vietnam. They should have the right to choose between the government established in Saigon under President Thieu and the Provisional Revolutionary Government.

The Provisional Revolutionary Government was set up by the National Liberation Front in 1969. Since them it had been recognized by a number of countries as the political organization of the guerrilla forces in conflict with the Saigon regime. One of the conditions of the ceasefire negotiations was that due recognition be given to the PRG by the United States and the government of South Vietnam. However, while they did formally recognize it in the terms of the agreement, in practice they did not accept its legitimacy. Significantly, it was rarely mentioned in certain Western news media: reports commonly referred to the 'Vietcong' or 'the communists'. It seems likely that, in the period after the ceasefire agreements, many people in the United States and in Britain still imagined that there was only one 'legitimate' authority in South Vietnam – the Saigon government.[3]

That was certainly the assumption made by Nixon's administration. On paper Nixon had accepted the right of the South Vietnamese to self-determination. By his actions, both before and after the agreement was signed, he attempted to ensure the continuance of Thieu's military dictatorship. From October 1972, when the plight of the South Vietnamese forces was critical, extra military supplies were sent to strengthen them. In November, Pentagon officials estimated that it would take two years to train the pilots and technicians needed to operate the new machines which were being delivered to the South Vietnamese Air Force – a body which experts believed would in the long run equal the USAF in its capacity to provide support for ground operations.[4] Meanwhile, suggested another official, the Vietnamese could bridge the pilot gap by employing 'contract personnel', by which he meant either active duty US pilots on loan to them or recently retired pilots of the USAF. Thanks to the United States, Thieu had, at the time of the ceasefire, some 550 combat aircraft and 1,100 helicopters. New weapons had also been delivered to the army which was able to contemplate the outbreak of peace behind the barrels of 2,500 artillery pieces and 800 tanks. In addition, Thieu's generals had at their disposal supplies sufficient to equip some two million soldiers.[5]

Shortly before the ceasefire went into effect the Saigon government produced a 'flurry of decrees' which negated its provisions. When the fighting ended the South Vietnamese people were in theory to be given an opportunity to decide their form of government. Thieu's new decrees were designed to deny them that choice by, for example, imprisoning 'neutralist and pro-communist elements', which in fact included any opponents of the regime. Even before the ceasefire there were waves of arrests and the paramilitary police were ordered to fire on anyone attempting to 'stir up trouble' among the population. Recognizing his lack of popular support, Thieu shed even the pretence of democracy, which had in any case been intended primarily to delude the American public, and his 'embattled authoritarian system . . . [appeared] in more honest colours'.[6]

The PRG, appreciating the political weakness of Saigon, issued millions of copies of the ceasefire agreements, which Thieu attempted to conceal from those under his rule. Both sides calculated that a genuine election would bring the downfall of Thieu.[7] At the same time, they both understood that there would be no such elections. Two weeks before the agreements were signed the PRG had adopted a 'national concord policy', inviting the co-operation of all the South Vietnamese people.[8] However,

peaceful co-existence as the only rational policy in a world stock-piled with nuclear weapons, the Chinese continued to stress the essential contradiction between popular revolutionary forces and anti-popular counter-revolutionary powers, in particular the USA and the Soviet Union. Peking gave strong verbal support to wars of national liberation and considered that Soviet policy was betraying the cause of international revolution. According to the Chinese, the two super-powers were colluding to divide the world between them: US imperialism and Soviet social imperialism were seen to be equally menacing.

While their conspiracy theory ignored the fundamental conflict of interest between the Soviet Union and the USA, it was true that the Soviet and American leaders had achieved some measure of *détente*. The tension created some years previously by the Cuban missile crisis had diminished and it did appear that in some areas the super-powers were anxious to preserve the status quo.[15] Certainly both were apprehensive about Chinese support for revolutionary movements which threatened to disturb the existing balance of power. Furthermore, both were prepared to invoke the 'yellow peril' in order to justify their own actions. In the United States, for example, advocates of a forward policy in Vietnam continually harped on the Chinese menace as the reason for American intervention.

That intervention did not at first substantially alter the pattern of relationships among the three powers although it did put some strain on the Soviet–American *détente*. Since the Soviet government claimed the leadership of the international communist movement, it could scarcely ignore the plight of North Vietnam, nor could it passively accept the extension of American influence in Southeast Asia. Even less could it afford to allow China, as a supporter of the Vietnamese revolutionaries, to pose as the centre of world revolution. Consequently the Soviets, like the Chinese, gave considerable military assistance to America's enemies in Vietnam. The fact that they were both supporting a fellow socialist state did not, however, reconcile them. While they saw clearly enough the danger that the US would seek to play each off against the other, they were unwilling to close ranks. On the contrary, the Chinese Cultural Revolution and the Soviet invasion of Czechoslovakia pushed them even farther apart.

Beginning in 1966, the Cultural Revolution cast China into

turmoil for the next three years. In addition to its enormous impact on the domestic scene it played havoc with China's foreign relations. Torn by internal conflicts, the Chinese became intensely hostile to all foreigners, including of course the Russians. In the midst of the upheaval the Soviet Union, in 1968, invaded another of its neighbours, Czechoslovakia. (It is worth noting that the Soviets, while aiding their brother socialists in North Vietnam, quickly snuffed out the campaign of their Czech comrades for another form of national liberation.) The invasion had a profound effect on the Chinese whose premier, Chou En-lai, declared that the 'Soviet revisionist clique of renegades [had] long since degenerated into a gang of social-imperialists and social-Fascists'.[16] During the following year the bitterness between the two countries went beyond the exchange of vitriolic abuse. Armed clashes between Soviet and Chinese frontier guards, causing considerable loss of life, occurred at a number of points on the border. In Moscow over 50,000 people marched past the Chinese Embassy throwing stones, lumps of ice, ink bottles and paint bombs.[17] The Chinese, for their part, began digging air-raid shelters against the possibility of a Soviet invasion.[18]

Such an intensification of the Sino–Soviet conflict worked to the advantage of the United States. Their *détente* with the USSR notwithstanding, much of American foreign policy was dominated by a global strategic adversary relationship with the Soviets. Thus it was convenient for them to have a quarter of the Soviet Union's highly modernized armed forces and a similar proportion of its nuclear weapons, immobilized near the Chinese border.[19] It was doubly useful in 1969 since by that year the effort of waging the Vietnam War was seriously weakening the US itself. World opinion was overwhelmingly hostile to the war. Furthermore the vast deployment of American military power was failing to achieve the desired result. Coupled to their lack of success was a growing financial crisis, largely a result of war expenditure, which added to the enormous domestic pressures and dislocation in the United States. In such a desperate situation the time seemed ripe for some change of direction for American policy in Asia.

Thus, during the next two years, the US government moved gradually towards a new relationship with the People's Republic of China. Kissinger, the principal negotiator, perceived a Sino–

US *détente* as a means of driving a new wedge between China and the Soviet Union, a move which, he felt, would put pressure on the North Vietnamese. According to him they were 'completely at the mercy of the Sino–Soviet dispute. If Communist China and the Soviet Union should clash ... Hanoi would be finished...'[20]

21. President Nixon with Chou En-lai on his visit to China in 1972.

An additional impetus towards a new approach to China was provided in 1971 by the United Nations' decision, despite US opposition, to admit Communist China and to exclude Taiwan,

America's ally, from the Security Council. The pragmatic Kissinger was not slow to appreciate the futility of trying to keep the Chinese isolated when world opinion had turned in favour of recognizing them. On their side, the Chinese leaders were willing partners in the negotiations. As the Soviet Union appeared ever more menacing, they sought a new tactic to respond to the threat. They saw that a *rapprochement* with the US would ensure that they were no longer threatened simultaneously by the two superpowers. Furthermore, they seemingly considered that they had more to fear from the Soviets than from the Americans. One authority has contended that the Chinese answered the overtures from Washington precisely because they thought that the American tide in Asia was on the ebb. In his opinion, while the Soviet–US *détente* was made possible by the success of containment in Europe, the Sino–US *détente* resulted from its failure in Asia.[21]

Whatever their antecedents, the outcome of the negotiations between Kissinger and the Chinese was Nixon's visit to the People's Republic in February 1972. A communiqué at the end of the visit stated, *inter alia*: 'There are essential differences between China and the United States in their social systems and foreign policies. However, the two sides agreed that countries, regardless of their social systems, should conduct their relations on the principles of respect for the sovereignty and territorial integrity of all States, non-aggression against other States, non-interference in the internal affairs of other States . . . Progress toward the normalization of relations between China and the United States is in the interests of all countries . . .'[22]

That communiqué testified to a dramatic volte face, particularly on the part of the US government. In effect, it invalidated a major reason for American intervention in Vietnam. As we have noted, the supporters of the war had constantly argued that a major military commitment was required to prevent Southeast Asia and, according to the domino theory, countries adjacent to that region, falling under the sway of Red China. However, at Peking, Nixon had agreed that the USA could co-exist peacefully with China and that international disputes could be settled without resorting to force. At the same time he tried to play down the significance of America's attempt to impose, by force of arms, its solution to the problems of Indochina. 'Vietnam,' he asserted, 'no longer distracts our attention from the fundamental issues of global diplomacy or diverts our energies from priorities at home.'[23] Kissinger later made a similar point: 'What we are doing now with China is so great, so historic, that the word "Vietnam" will be only a footnote when it is written in history.'[24]

It was natural for such men to turn a blind eye to their military débâcle and to magnify their diplomatic triumph. Less partial observers may find it much harder to dismiss so lightly the bloody war that the Americans waged for so long in Indochina. They are likely to conclude that, while there were many pressures for a *détente* with China, the most weighty was the failure of the US to defeat its enemies in Vietnam.

There can be no doubt that a military victory would have reinforced the hard-liners in Washington. Particularly in the United States, nothing succeeds like success. The crushing of resistance south of the seventeenth parallel would have prompted the more hawkish generals to urge an invasion of the North – a move which some favoured even when the war was going badly for them. In the euphoria of victory there would have been no likelihood of a more conciliatory approach to China. Almost certainly the Chinese would have refused to consider any negotiation, in the unlikely event of its being proposed, with an American leadership flushed with victory. Thus it appears that the conditions for Nixon's Peking visit, which he described with characteristic modesty as 'a week that changed the world', were created not so much by Kissinger's diplomatic wizardry as by the military prowess of his Vietnamese adversaries. While a more definitive assessment of the Vietnam War must be left to future historians, it is inconceivable that they will relegate it to a footnote.

The process whereby the US leaders began to appreciate that they could not easily dominate Southeast Asia was long and painful. The price was paid above all by the people of Vietnam and their neighbours in Cambodia and Laos. We have already indicated the horrendous loss of life, the injuries from napalm and other 'anti-personnel' weapons and the devastation both of the countryside and the towns. The death and destruction was intended to extirpate revolutionary movements which, by removing power from the privileged classes in their societies, would also weaken the influence of the United States, on whose support those groups depended. In practice US intervention reinforced the revolutionaries by threatening to destroy completely the societies which the Americans claimed to be saving from communism. It helped to forge an alliance of the NLF in Vietnam, the Khmer Rouge in Cambodia and the Pathet Lao in Laos. Even in Thailand, which throughout the war had been a stronghold of US influence, the ruling military clique has come under attack. The indications are that Southeast Asia is much less amenable to American pressure than it was before the Vietnam War.

In South Vietnam itself the fighting has continued with the odds mounting against President Thieu. As pressure in the US Congress to check the flow of dollars to Vietnam increases so does the strength of the revolutionaries. Resistance to the Saigon government by non-communist groups is also on the upsurge. Both external and internal pressures are sapping the strength of Thieu's army. Even so it is possible that the war will persist for some time: peace has remained tragically elusive in Vietnam. Whenever the military conflict does end there will be a new war to win – the war against the misery and the devastation which have resulted from the struggle of an Asian people to determine its own destiny.

Postscript, May 1975

The reconstruction of Vietnam began sooner than anyone had anticipated. In January 1975 the North Vietnamese 7th Division captured Phuoc Binh. Encouraged by that success, in March the NVA and PRG forces attacked a number of other provincial capitals which, as one Western journalist noted, were capitals with no province left. On 17 March Ban Me Thuot, the regional administrative centre of the Central Highlands, was occupied. Thieu ordered his troops to withdraw from the Highlands to concentrate on the defence of Saigon. While one leader writer claimed that military victory for the communists was still a distant prospect,[25] the withdrawal soon degenerated into a panic flight. The loss, in rapid succession, of major cities testified to the disintegration of South Vietnam's army. Hué was abandoned without a fight on 26 March. The NLF guerrillas and the North Vietnamese marched into Da Nang on 30 March and took Qui Nhon on 1 April.

On the same day Lon Nol, the US protégé in Cambodia, fled to Indonesia. The Khmer Rouge occupied the capital, Phnom Penh, on 17 April, thus undermining further the morale of the regime in Saigon. Nevertheless, Thieu hoped that, despite their acceptance of the loss of Cambodia, the Americans would continue to prop up South Vietnam by airlifting more supplies. President Ford, Nixon's successor, did request authority to spend an additional $1,000 million. Congress, aware that their ally had abandoned at least that amount of military equipment to the communists during March and anxious to avoid extra entanglement, turned a deaf ear. Any prospect that it might relent faded when Thieu resigned on 21 April. In a long, rambling speech he reiterated his claim that Nixon had, in January 1973, secretly promised actively to intervene, if need be, to protect South Vietnam and bitterly enquired: 'Is an American's word reliable these days?'[26]

Denied the support of a new US military effort, the South Vietnamese sought to 'save Saigon' by using an ingenious product of American technology, the CBU 55 bomb. A so-called 'depression' bomb, its effect was to suck up oxygen over a radius of 250 yards for long enough to kill all human life. Enemy troops killed by such weapons were found with their mouths open, clutching their throats as though gasping for breath.[27] On 24 April the PRG accused the US and Saigon governments of 'flouting all the norms of morality and international law' in using chemical bombs that caused instant asphyxiation.[28] This new tactic provided a sharp reminder of what the London *Times* referred to as the 'human cost of a brutal bloodbath'. In an article on 25 April it pointed out that, according to the Indo-Chinese Resource Centre in Washington, the total casualties, dead and wounded, from January 1961 to January 1975 was 5,773,190. Excluding US losses, that figure represented more than 10 per cent of the population of Cambodia, Laos and both North and South Vietnam. The dead totalled 2,122,244, including 56,231 Americans.

During the final phase of the conflict there were in fact remarkably few casualties. Panic rather than communist attacks led to the collapse of government positions. Despite fears to the contrary, there was no 'bloodbath' in the areas occupied by the PRG.[29] Further loss of life in Saigon itself was averted by the emergence of leaders prepared to yield to the inevitable. General Duong Van Minh replaced Tran Van Huong, Thieu's immediate successor, as President on 28 April and announced that he would immediately seek to negotiate a ceasefire and peace terms. On the following day the Americans at last departed from Saigon in a massive evacuation by helicopter. A few hours after their frenzied withdrawal Minh capitulated. On the eve of May Day barefoot teenage guerrillas and hardened regular troops in jungle battle dress were greeted by cheering citizens of Saigon, which was renamed Ho Chi Minh City.[30]

DIENBIENPHU

Dienbienphu was situated near the border with Laos in a large valley which produced some 2,000 tons of rice per year and was an important centre for the processing of opium, a commodity traded on the black market by the Vietminh in exchange for US weapons and medical supplies. At the junction of a road network, it was, according to Giap, a 'strategic position of first importance, capable of becoming an infantry and air base of extreme efficiency'.

The French had lost control of Dienbienphu at the end of November 1952. On 2 November 1953 General Navarre, the French commander-in-chief, ordered its reoccupation by a date not later than 1 December. General Cogny, designated commander of the operation, felt it was misconceived but was later reconciled to attempting to use Dienbienphu as a 'mooring point' for guerrilla warfare against the Vietminh. While Cogny feared that Dienbienphu would become a 'battalion meat-grinder', Colonel Nicot, the officer commanding air transport, warned Navarre that it would be impossible to maintain a constant flow of supplies to the valley which, although it possessed a small Japanese-built airstrip, was 200 miles distant from the main French base at Hanoi. Nevertheless, on 20 November, Operation Castor was launched and within a few days French paratroops had dislodged the enemy and secured the position.

Giap decided to 'wipe out at all costs' the whole enemy force at Dienbienphu. As he began to concentrate his divisions it became clear that the 'mooring point' concept would have to be abandoned. On 3 December Navarre ordered his troops to prepare for a pitched defensive battle, believing that their superior discipline and firepower would overwhelm the enemy and thus tilt the military balance throughout the country in favour of the French. The Vietminh accepted his challenge and made elaborate counter-moves. Rejecting the notion of a rapidly mounted assault before the French were fully prepared, Giap opted for a policy of attrition. In addition, he carried out a number of diversionary operations to disperse the enemy's reserves.

During the next three months the Vietminh performed a remarkable logistical feat. Hundreds of thousands of porters, using reinforced bicycles to carry loads of 450 lb, supplied Giap's soldiers with food, guns and ammunition from China. Guns were dragged inch by inch at night into emplacements tunnelled out of the hills surrounding the valley, enabling their crews to fire straight down at the French positions, including the airstrip. Anti-aircraft guns were also cunningly sited and used to devastating effect. In addition, an elaborate system of trenches, dug at great speed, brought the Vietminh to within a few yards of the French outposts; the endless noise of their digging helped to demoralize the enemy.

On 13 March 1954 Giap launched his offensive. As his barrage smashed the enemy strongpoints Colonel Piroth, the French artillery commander, realizing how tragically he had under-estimated the Vietminh firepower, committed suicide with a hand grenade. For fifty-six days and nights the French resisted heroic-ally in abominable conditions. Exceptionally heavy rains in April swamped their positions, they were short of ammunition and, in the last weeks of the battle, many were fighting on half rations. Even so they inflicted heavy casualties and Giap was obliged to make a special effort to maintain the morale of his own men.

However, by 6 May the French were confined to a space the size of two football pitches when Giap deployed his Russian Katyusha rockets to strike the final blows. On 7 May the French command post was overrun and the garrison was forced to surrender. One day after the loss of Dienbienphu the French delegation at the Geneva Conference sued for peace in Indochina.

Bibliographical note
The bare outline offered here can best be supplemented by reading B. Fall, *Hell in a Very Small Place* (Pall Mall Press, 1967). For an interesting account of the part played by Giap, see R. J. O'Neill, *General Giap: Politician and Strategist* (Cassell Australia, 1969).

REFERENCES

CHAPTER ONE

1. R. Smith, *Viet-Nam and the West*, p. 4.
2. Quoted in S. E. Ambrose, *Rise to Globalism*, p. 322.
3. F. Fitzgerald, *Fire in the Lake*, p. 9.
4. See J. Buttinger, *Vietnam: A Political History*, p. 162; D. G. E. Hall, *A History of South-East Asia*, p. 786.
5. Hall, op. cit., pp. 789–90.
6. Ibid., pp. 786–8; M. E. Gettleman (ed.), *Vietnam, History, Documents, and Opinions on a major world crisis*, p. 30.
7. Buttinger, op. cit., p. 162.
8. R. Smith, 'The Development of Opposition to French Rule in Southern Vietnam 1880–1940', *Past & Present* No. 54, February 1972, p. 94.
9. See M. Osborne, *Region of Revolt: Focus on Southeast Asia*, pp. 41–5.
10. See Buttinger, op. cit., pp. 155–60.
11. In the words of Lord Curzon, their victories 'reverberated through the whispering galleries of the East'.
12. That is, unpaid labour demanded of a tenant by his landlord – a relic of a feudal system.
13. Buttinger, op. cit., p. 158.
14. For a useful biography, see J. Lacouture, *Ho Chi Minh*.
15. Lacouture, op. cit., p. 31.
16. Ibid., p. 32.
17. Ibid.
18. For its programme, see Gettleman, op. cit., pp. 39–41.
19. Buttinger, op. cit., p. 180.
20. Ibid., pp. 175–7.
21. See Smith, *Past & Present* No. 54, p. 129.
22. Osborne, op. cit., p. 63.
23. See B. Fall's comment on his 'hammering away at concrete problems, never bothering with doctrine.', quoted in D. Landau, *Kissinger: The Uses of Power*, p. 161.

CHAPTER TWO

1. Signed in August 1939, it was a non-aggression pact between Germany and the Soviet Union. The Indo-chinese Communist Party, like other communist parties throughout the world, was expected to follow Stalin's line. Hence they could not attack Japan, which was an ally of Nazi Germany.
2. J. Woddis (ed.), *Ho Chi Minh, Selected Articles and Speeches 1920–67*, p. 30.
3. Lacouture, op. cit., p. 68.

4. Smith, *Viet-Nam and the West*, p. 110.
5. See Osborne, op. cit., pp. 58–9.
6. Ian McDonald, 'Ho Chi Minh praised by US intelligence in 1945 as non-communist patriot', *The Times*, 26 February 1973.
7. Ibid.
8. Lacouture, op. cit., pp. 97–8.
9. Gettleman, op. cit., pp. 63–6.
10. Quoted in Lacouture, op. cit., p. 92.
11. Quoted in A. M. Schlesinger Jr., *The Bitter Heritage, Vietnam and American Democracy 1941–66*, p. 11.
12. Ibid., pp. 11–12.
13. G. Rosie, *The British in Vietnam*, p. 51.
14. Ibid., pp. 62–3.
15. Quoted in E. Snow, *The Other Side of the River*, p. 686.
16. Rosie, op. cit., p. 96.
17. Ibid., p. 105.
18. See *Keesings Contemporary Archives*, Vol. VI, p. 7779.
19. Rosie, op. cit., p. 140.
20. D. Lancaster, *The Emancipation of French Indo-China*, p. 127.
21. E. J. Hammer, *The Struggle for Indochina*, pp. 145–6.
22. Quoted in Lacouture, op. cit., p. 104.
23. Quoted in Gettleman, op. cit., p. 70.
24. See Lacouture, op. cit., p. 119.
25. Admiral Thierry d'Argenlieu was French High Commissioner in Indochina.
26. Lacouture, op. cit., p. 149.
27. A. Werth, *France 1940–55*, p. 346.
28. Ibid., p. 447.
29. N. Sheehan *et al.*, *The Pentagon Papers*, p. 9.
30. Ibid.
31. Ibid., pp. 9–10.
32. Gettleman, op. cit., p. 85.
33. B. Fall, *The Two Viet-Nams*, p. 113.
34. For a comprehensive account see J. Roy, *The Battle of Dienbienphu*.
35. See Gettleman, op. cit., p. 119.
36. Sheehan, op. cit., p. 40.
37. Ibid.

CHAPTER THREE

1. See Osborne, op. cit., ch. 6 *Malaya and the Philippines: Two Revolts that Failed*.
2. Ibid., p. 110.
3. Gettleman, op. cit., p. 161.
4. Lacouture, op. cit., p. 168 fn. 2.
5. Fitzgerald, op. cit., p. 69.
6. Lacouture, op. cit., p. 168.
7. Woddis, op. cit., p. 90.
8. D. Eisenhower, *Mandate for Change*, p. 372.
9. See Sheehan, op. cit., pp. 15–19; ibid., pp. 53ff.
10. Ibid., p. 14.
11. For comment on the Truman Doctrine, see H. Higgins, *The Cold War*, pp. 43–6.
12. Gettleman, op. cit., p. 215.
13. Sheehan, op. cit., pp. 19ff.

14. See R. Scheer, *The Genesis of United States Support for Ngo Dinh Diem*, in Gettleman, op. cit., pp. 246–64.
15. D. Warner, *The Last Confucian*, p. 196.
16. See B. S. N. Murti, *Vietnam Divided*, pp. 157–9.
17. See R. Scigliano, *South Vietnam: Nation Under Stress*, pp. 133–4.
18. See N. Chomsky, *The Backroom Boys*, p. 112.
19. Fitzgerald, op. cit., p. 85.
20. Sheehan, op. cit., p. 21.
21. Ibid., pp. 23–4.
22. US State Department, *A Threat to Peace*, pp. 5–7.
23. Sheehan, op. cit., pp. 70–2.
24. M. Taylor, 'South Vietnam: Lavish aid limited progress, Pacific Affairs 1961', quoted in R. Murray (ed.), *Vietnam*, pp. 54–5.
25. F. Greene, *The Enemy*, p. 112.
26. Ibid., p. 113.
27. Gettleman, op. cit., p. 238.
28. Fitzgerald, op. cit., p. 90.
29. See P. Devillers, 'Mistakes of the Diem Government', *China Quarterly*, January–March 1962.
30. Sheehan, op. cit., p. 72.
31. Fitzgerald, op. cit., p. 95.
32. Ibid., pp. 126–7.
33. Ibid.
34. See *Keesings Research Report, South Vietnam, A Political History 1954–70*, pp. 28–9.
35. Such was the view taken in the State Department paper 'A Threat to Peace'.

CHAPTER FOUR

1. T. Draper, *Abuse of Power, U.S. Foreign Policy from Cuba to Vietnam*, p. 44.
2. B. Fall, quoted in N. Chomsky, *At War with Asia*, p. 220.
3. See Chomsky, *The Backroom Boys*, n. 30 pp. 175–6; also, Chomsky, *At War with Asia*, p. 219 and n. 9 pp. 278–9.
4. *Keesings Contemporary Archives*, Vol. XI, p. 15349B.
5. Fitzgerald, op. cit., pp. 223–4.
6. Chomsky, *At War with Asia*, p. 219.
7. Fall, *The Two Viet-Nams*, pp. 160–1.
8. Buttinger, op. cit., pp. 423–4.
9. Gettleman, op. cit., p. 230.
10. Ibid., p. 231.
11. Ibid., p. 230 n. 8.
12. W. Burchett, *Vietnam: Inside Story of the Guerilla War*, pp. 112–14.
13. Lacouture, op. cit., pp. 240–1; Chomsky, *The Backroom Boys*, pp. 127–8.
14. Gettleman, op. cit., pp. 236–7.
15. Ibid., p. 239; Lacouture, 'Le Monde', 15 April 1965, quoted in Murray, *Vietnam*, pp. 121–2; Lacouture, op. cit., p. 241; Draper, op. cit., p. 52.
16. Gettleman, op. cit., p. 239.
17. N. Chomsky, *American Power and the New Mandarins*, p. 233 n. 75; Smith, *Viet-Nam and the West*, pp. 165–6.
18. Chomsky, *American Power and the New Mandarins*, p. 195, pp. 225–6.
19. Fitzgerald, op. cit., p. 148.
20. Sheehan, op. cit., p. 69.
21. For agrovilles, see below, pp. 50–1.

22. D. Halberstam, *The Making of a Quagmire*, p. 63. But see also Chomsky, *The Backroom Boys*, p. 127, where he quotes a use of 'Viet Cong' from May 1959.
23. Buttinger, op. cit., p. 459.
24. For the Front's programme, see Gettleman, op. cit., pp. 265–9.
25. See above, pp. 37–8.
26. Buttinger, op. cit., pp. 434–7.
27. Fitzgerald, op. cit., pp. 148–9.
28. Sheehan, op. cit., p. 86.

CHAPTER FIVE

1. Chomsky, *The Backroom Boys*, p. 125.
2. Sheehan, op. cit., pp. 79 and 82.
3. D. Halberstam, *The Best and the Brightest*, pp. 122–4.
4. Sheehan, op. cit., p. 142.
5. Draper, op. cit., p. 58.
6. See Chomsky, *The Backroom Boys*, p. 9, n. 4 pp. 178–9.
7. See above, p. 30.
8. Sheehan, op. cit., p. 79.
9. Halberstam, *The Best and the Brightest*, p. 299.
10. Ibid., pp. 209–11.
11. Homer Bigart, quoted in Halberstam, *The Making of a Quagmire*, p. 75.
12. See above, pp. 26–7.
13. Quoted in Chomsky, *The Backroom Boys*, p. 8.
14. Halberstam, *The Making of a Quagmire*, p. 186.
15. Chomsky, *The Backroom Boys*, p. 9.
16. Fitzgerald, op. cit., pp. 10–11.
17. Hilsman, quoted in Chomsky, *The Backroom Boys*, p. 8; see also Chomsky, *American Power and the New Mandarins*, p. 205.
18. Sheehan, op. cit., p. 155.
19. Fitzgerald, op. cit., p. 125.
20. Halberstam, *The Best and the Brightest*, p. 186.
21. Ibid., p. 249.
22. Halberstam, *The Making of a Quagmire*, p. 202.
23. Ibid., p. 211.
24. Buttinger, op. cit., p. 466.
25. Halberstam, *The Making of a Quagmire*, p. 199.
26. See Halberstam, *The Best and the Brightest*, pp. 259–62.
27. Sheehan, op. cit., p. 167.
28. Ibid.
29. Ibid., p. 166.
30. Ibid., pp. 194–5.
31. Ibid., p. 197.
32. Ibid., p. 173.
33. Halberstam, *The Best and the Brightest*, p. 265.
34. Sheehan, op. cit., p. 174.
35. A. M. Schlesinger Jr., *A Thousand Days*, p. 845; Halberstam, *The Best and the Brightest*, p. 272.
36. Sheehan, op. cit., p. 178.
37. Ibid., pp. 230–1.

CHAPTER SIX

1. Halberstam, *The Best and the Brightest*, p. 298.
2. Sheehan, op. cit., p. 233.
3. Ibid., pp. 271ff.
4. Ibid., p. 276.
5. Ibid., p. 241.
6. Ibid., p. 233.
7. Quoted in Murray, *Vietnam*, p. 111.
8. Chomsky, *The Backroom Boys*, p. 133.
9. Draper, op. cit., p. 96.
10. For his reply see Gettleman, op. cit., pp. 335–41.
11. See comments on *The Mysterious 325th* in Draper, op. cit., pp. 77–86.
12. Chomsky, *The Backroom Boys*, pp. 130–1.
13. Halberstam, *The Best and the Brightest*, p. 404.
14. Sheehan, op. cit., p. 278.
15. Ibid.
16. See comment by Chomsky, *American Power and the New Mandarins*, pp. 209–10; for further information on McNamara's report see Halberstam, *The Best and the Brightest*, pp. 353–5.
17. Sheehan, op. cit., pp. 247–9.
18. See below p. 65.
19. Sheehan, op. cit., p. 256.
20. Ibid., p. 258.
21. See ibid., pp. 258ff.; Halberstam, *The Best and the Brightest*, pp. 411ff.
22. Sheehan, op. cit., pp. 264–5.
23. Halberstam, *The Best and the Brightest*, p. 417.
24. W. Warbey, *Ho Chi Minh*, p. 172.
25. Halberstam, *The Best and the Brightest*, p. 414.
26. Ibid., pp. 411–12.
27. Sheehan, op. cit., p. 265.
28. Warbey, op. cit., p. 172.
29. In his customary down-to-earth language, Johnson gloated to journalists on 5 August: 'I didn't just screw Ho Chi Minh. I cut his pecker off.' Halberstam, *The Best and the Brightest*, p. 414.
30. Sheehan, op. cit., p. 311.
31. Ibid., pp. 315, 360.
32. Ibid., p. 320.
33. Ibid., p. 336.
34. Ibid., p. 338.
35. Ibid., p. 343.
36. J. Cameron, *Witness*, p. 66.
37. Ibid., p. 67.
38. Chomsky, *American Power and the New Mandarins*, p. 184.
39. Chomsky, *At War with Asia*, p. 227.
40. Sheehan, op. cit., p. 386.
41. Halberstam, *The Best and the Brightest*, p. 599.
42. Sheehan, op. cit., p. 416.
43. Ibid., p. 467.
44. Halberstam, *The Best and the Brightest*, p. 618.
45. Chomsky, *The Backroom Boys*, pp. 98–9; Halberstam, *The Best and the Brightest*, p. 652.
46. Chomsky, *The Backroom Boys*, p. 99.
47. Sheehan, op. cit., p. 592.

48. Ibid., p. 601; Halberstam, *The Best and the Brightest*, p. 653.
49. Sheehan, op. cit., p. 611.

CHAPTER SEVEN

1. Gettleman, op. cit., pp. 341ff. For a less altruistic version of US motives, see McNaughton's memorandum in Sheehan, op. cit., p. 255. See also Chomsky, *For Reasons of State*, p. 235.
2. Paul Johnson, 'America's Suez?', *New Statesman*, 9 February 1968.
3. Chomsky, *The Backroom Boys*, p. 93.
4. Ibid., p. 85.
5. US pilots were involved before 1965; see Chomsky, *The Backroom Boys*, p. 9.
6. Chomsky, *The Backroom Boys*, p. 93.
7. See F. Harvey, *Air War – Vietnam*, ch. 15.
8. Chomsky, *The Backroom Boys*, p. 25.
9. R. A. Falk, G. Kolko, R. J. Lifton (eds.), *Crimes of War*, pp. 411–12.
10. Ibid., p. 411.
11. Ibid., p. 412.
12. Ibid., p. 413.
13. Chomsky, *For Reasons of State*, p. 226; Chomsky, *At War with Asia*, p. 74.
14. Chomsky, *For Reasons of State*, pp. 225–6.
15. See above p. 59.
16. Falk *et al.*, op. cit., p. 288.
17. Ibid., p. 286.
18. Ibid., p. 285.
19. Chomsky, *American Power and the New Mandarins*, p. 254 n. 2.
20. Ibid., p. 255.
21. Falk *et al.*, op. cit., pp. 278–9.
22. Ibid., p. 279.
23. Ibid., pp. 332–3.
24. Ibid., p. 358.
25. Chomsky, *For Reasons of State*, p. 223.
26. Ibid., p. 225.
27. Ibid., pp. 235–6.
28. See R. Hammer, *One Morning in the War, The Tragedy at Pinkville*, p. 197.
29. M. McCarthy, *Vietnam*, p. 55.
30. Buttinger, op. cit., p. 492.
31. Halbertsam, *The Best and the Brightest*, p. 483.
32. For numerous examples see passim W. J. Lederer, *The Anguished American*.
33. Fitzgerald, op. cit., pp. 311–12.
34. Lederer, op. cit., p. 39.
35. Chomsky, *At War with Asia*, pp. 52–3.
36. Chomsky, *The Backroom Boys*, p. 151.
37. Lodge, for example, regarded the Buddhists 'as equivalent to card-carrying Communists.' Chomsky, *The Backroom Boys*, p. 118.
38. Chomsky, *American Power and the New Mandarins*, p. 108 n. 25.
39. Fitzgerald, op. cit., p. 252.
39. Ibid., pp. 349–50.
41. Chomsky, *American Power and the New Mandarins*, pp. 38–9; Draper, op. cit., p. 103.
42. Fitzgerald, op. cit., p. 139.

43. Ibid., p. 195.
44. Ibid., p. 169.
45. Draper, op. cit., p. 97.
46. Buttinger, op. cit., p. 487.
47. Chomsky, *The Backroom Boys*, p. 82.
48. Ibid.
49. Sheehan, op. cit., pp. 550–1; Halberstam, *The Best and the Brightest*, p. 643.
50. Simon Winchester, 'LBJ sanctioned secret bombing', *The Guardian*, 10 August 1973.

CHAPTER EIGHT

1. Halberstam, *The Best and the Brightest*, p. 512.
2. Ibid., p. 530.
3. See Draper, op. cit., pp. 16–21.
4. C. Reich, *The Greening of America*, p. 194.
5. Quoted in Snow, op. cit., p. 709.
6. Quoted in J. Bosch, *Pentagonism, A Substitute for Imperialism*, p. 9.
7. Ibid., p. 10.
8. Ibid., p. 115.
9. Halberstam, *The Best and the Brightest*, p. 645.
10. Buttinger, op. cit., pp. 489–90.
11. See J. J. Zasloff & A. E. Goodman (eds.), *Indochina in Conflict, A Political Assessment*, p. 205.
12. Bosch, op. cit., p. 37.
13. For a comment on élites see Chomsky, *At War with Asia*, p. 26.
14. Buttinger, op. cit., p. 490.
15. Fitzgerald, op. cit., p. 303.
16. Halberstam, *The Best and the Brightest*, p. 609.
17. Buttinger, op. cit., p. 490.
18. Ibid., p. 491.
19. Ibid., pp. 490–1.
20. R. Segal, *America's Receding Future*, p. 250.
21. Ibid., pp. 260–1.
22. See N. Mailer, *The Armies of the Night*, pp. 296–7.
23. Chomsky, *American Power and the New Mandarins*, p. 316.
24. Schlesinger, *The Bitter Heritage*, p. 121.
25. Ibid., p. 49.
26. Ibid., p. 144.
27. Ibid., p. 52.
28. Chomsky, *At Wat with Asia*, pp. 62–3.
29. Chomsky, *The Backroom Boys*, p. 78.
30. Chomsky, *American Power and the New Mandarins*, p. 12.
31. Bosch, op. cit., p. 12.
32. Ibid., p. 85.
33. Ibid., p. 68.
34. Ibid., p. 5.
35. Halberstam, *The Best and the Brightest*, p. 640.
36. Fitzgerald, op. cit., p. 394.
37. Halberstam, *The Best and the Brightest*, p. 648.
38. Ibid., p. 662.

CHAPTER NINE

1. Fitzgerald, op. cit., p. 403.
2. Ibid., p. 468 n. 15.
3. Don Oberdorfer, quoted in D. Halberstam, 'The Reign of Lyndon B. Nixonger', *New Statesman*, 19 May 1972.
4. See L. Heren, *No Hail, No Farewell*, p. 226.
5. Fitzgerald, op. cit., p. 406 n. 2.
6. Ibid., pp. 406–7.
7. Ibid., p. 405.
8. Ibid., p. 407.
9. Quoted in R. West, 'Vietnam: The Year of the Rat', *New Statesman*, 25 February 1972.
10. Chomsky, *The Backroom Boys*, pp. 199–200.
11. Ibid., p. 104.
12. Fitzgerald, op. cit., p. 418.
13. Chomsky, *At War with Asia*, p. 116.
14. N. Sihanouk & W. Burchett, *My War With the CIA*, p. 52.
15. Leading article, 'Mr. Nixon's private wars', *The Guardian*, 6 August 1973.
16. Sihanouk & Burchett, op. cit., p. 59.
17. Ibid., p. 259.
18. Ibid., pp. 170–1
19. Chomsky, *At War with Asia*, p. 179.
20. Ibid., p. 273.
21. Sheehan, op. cit., p. 239.
22. Simon Winchester, 'LBJ sanctioned secret bombing', *The Guardian*, 10 August 1973.
23. Leading article, 'Mr. Nixon's private wars', *The Guardian*, 6 August 1973; article, 'Nixon "lied" over raids into Laos', *The Guardian*, 13 August 1973.
24. Peter Dale Scott, 'Laos: The Story Nixon Won't Tell', *New York Review of Books*, 9 April 1970, p. 39. Scott quotes another source suggesting that 20,000 sorties were being flown per month, see n. 28.
25. Chomsky, *At War with Asia*, p. 195.
26. Ibid.
27. Chomsky, *The Backroom Boys*, p. 37.
28. See H. Arendt, *Crises of the Republic*, pp. 9ff.
29. See Halberstam, *The Best and the Brightest*, pp. 409–10.
30. See R. Hammer, *One Morning in the War*.
31. Chomsky, *At War with Asia*, p. 81.
32. Fitzgerald, op. cit., p. 377.
33. R. Hammer, op. cit., p. 175.
34. Ibid., pp. 197ff.
35. Falk *et al.*, op. cit., p. 466.
36. Chomsky, *For Reasons of State*, p. 224.
37. Falk *et al.*, op. cit., pp. 466–7.
38. Chomsky, *At War with Asia*, pp. 232–3.
39. Chomsky, *American Power and the New Mandarins*, p. 224; Chomsky, *The Backroom Boys*, p. 129; Falk *et al.*, op. cit., p. 265.
40. Chomsky, *At War with Asia*, p. 234.
41. R. West, 'Vietnam: The Year of the Rat', *New Statesman*, 25 February 1972.
42. J. Fox, 'Vietnamisation: The price they had to pay', *Sunday Times Magazine*, 25 June 1972.
43. Article, 'The failure of American bombing', *Sunday Times*, 7 May 1972.
44. Gavin Young, 'Now that the GIs have gone', *Observer*, 1 April 1973.
45. R. West, *Vietnam: The Year of the Rat*.

46. Zasloff & Goodman, op. cit., p. 219.
47. J. Fox, *Vietnamisation: The price they had to pay.*
48. Ibid.
49. R. Littauer, 'Twenty million dollars of death a day', *The Times*, 26 May 1972.
50. Anthony Lewis, 'What they talk about when B52s pound Hanoi', *Observer*, 18 June 1972.
51. Marc Ribou & Sven Oste, 'Giant-Killers', *Observer Magazine*, 17 December 1972.
52. Ibid.
53. Anthony Lewis, 'Widening cracks in Dr. Kissinger's facade', *The Times*, 20 December 1972. See also a pamphlet, *The British Press and Vietnam*, published by the Indochina Solidarity conference.
54. Alex Finer, 'Why B52s are in trouble', *Sunday Times*, 24 December 1972.
55. Jean Leclerc du Sablon & Jean Thoraval, 'Hanoi survives in its "caves"', *Sunday Times*, 31 December 1972.
56. Letter in *The Times*, 30 December 1972.
57. Michael Allen, 'How it feels to be bombed in Hanoi', *Sunday Times*, 31 December 1972.
58. Alex Finer, *Why B52s are in trouble.*
59. See Chomsky, *The Backroom Boys*, p. 160.

CHAPTER TEN

1. See above, pp. 27–8.
2. Chomsky, *The Backroom Boys*, p. 158.
3. See *The British Press in Vietnam*, p. 24.
4. Chomsky, *The Backroom Boys*, p. 171.
5. Murray Sayle, 'Lyrical words from Paris sound like a sick joke in Saigon', *Sunday Times*, 28 January 1973.
6. Ibid.
7. Mark Frankland, 'After the ceasefire, the closed fist v the out-stretched hand', *Observer*, 28 January 1973; Chomsky, *The Backroom Boys*, pp. 154–5.
8. Ibid.
9. Quoted in Jon Swain, 'The Year of the Ceasefire: every week 1,000 Vietnamese are killed', *Sunday Times*, 27 January 1974.
10. Frankland, 'After the ceasefire, the closed fist v the out-stretched hand', *Observer*, 28 January 1973.
11. Heren, op. cit., p. 268.
12. Frankland, 'After the ceasefire, the closed fist v the out-stretched hand', *Observer*, 28 January 1973.
13. Henry Brandon, 'Now America tries to forget the war that had no heroes', *Sunday Times*, 28 January 1973.
14. Landau, op. cit., pp. xvi–xvii.
15. See Higgins, *The Cold War*, pp. 121–2.
16. *Keesings Contemporary Archives*, Vol. XVI, p. 22996.
17. *Keesings Research Report, The Sino–Soviet Dispute (1970)*, p. 117.
18. K. Mehnert, *China Today*, p. 229.
19. M. B. Yahuda, 'China's New Era of International Relations', *Political Quarterly* Vol. 43 No. 3, p. 301.
20. Landau, op. cit., p. 212.
21. Yahuda, op. cit., p. 307.
22. *Keesings Contemporary Archives*, Vol. XVIII, p. 25150.
23. Landau, op. cit., p. 245.
24. Ibid., p. 244.

25. *The Times*, 20 March 1975.
26. *The Times*, 22 April 1975.
27. *The Times*, 24 April 1975.
28. *The Times*, 25 April 1975.
29. Jean Thoraval, 'Invaders of Da Nang Commended', *The Times*, 24 April 1975.
30. *The Times*, 1 May 1975.

BIBLIOGRAPHY

Ambrose, S. E., *Rise to Globalism* (Allen Lane, 1971)
Arendt, H., *Crises of the Republic* (Penguin, 1973)

Bator, V., *Vietnam, A Diplomatic Tragedy: Origins of U.S. Involvement* (Faber & Faber, 1967)
Bosch, J., *Pentagonism, a substitute for imperialism* (Grove Press, 1968)
Burchett, W., *Vietnam: Inside Story of the Guerrilla War* (International Publishers, 1954)
Buttinger, J., *Vietnam: A Political History* (André Deutsch, 1969)

Cameron, J., *Witness* (V. Gollancz, 1966)
Chomsky, N., *American Power and the New Mandarins* (Penguin, 1969)
  At War with Asia (Fontana/Collins, 1971)
  The Backroom Boys (Fontana/Collins, 1973)
  For Reasons of State (Fontana/Collins, 1973)

Draper, T., *Abuse of Power, U.S. Foreign Policy from Cuba to Vietnam* (Penguin, 1969)

Eisenhower, D. D., *Mandate for Change* (Heinemann, 1963)

Falk, R. A., *Vietnam and International Law* (O'Hare, 1967)
Falk, R. A., Kolko, G., Lifton, R. J. (eds.), *Crimes of War* (Vintage Books, 1971)
Fall, B., *The Two Viet-Nams* (Pall Mall Press, 1965)
  Viet-Nam Witness (Pall Mall Press, 1966)
Fenn, C., *Ho Chi Minh* (Studio Vista, 1973)
Fitzgerald, F., *Fire in the Lake* (Macmillan, 1972)
Fulbright, J. W., *The Arrogance of Power* (Penguin, 1970)

Gerassi, J., *North Vietnam: A Documentary* (Allen & Unwin, 1968)
Gettleman, M. E. (ed.), *Vietnam, History, Documents, and Opinions on a Major World Crisis* (Penguin, 1966)

Giap, Vo Nguyen, *Big Victory, Great Task* (Frederick Praeger, 1968)
Greene, F., *Vietnam! Vietnam!* (J. Cape, 1967)
  The Enemy (J. Cape, 1970)

Halberstam, D., *The Making of a Quagmire* (Bodley Head, 1965)
  The Best and the Brightest (Barrie & Jenkins, 1972)
Hall, D. G. E., *A History of South-East Asia* (Macmillan, 1968)
Hammer, E. J., *The Struggle for Indochina* (Stanford University Press, 1954)
Hammer, R., *One Morning in the War, The Tragedy at Pinkville* (Rupert Hart-Davis, 1970)
Harvey, F., *Air War – Vietnam* (Bantam, 1967)
Heren, L., *No Hail, No Farewell* (Weidenfeld & Nicolson, 1970)
Higgins, H., *The Cold War* (Heinemann Educational Books, 1974)

Indochina Solidarity Conference, *The British Press and Vietnam* (1973)

Keesing's Research Report,
  South Vietnam, A Political History (Scribners, 1970)
Kiernan, V. G., *The Lords of Human Kind* (Penguin, 1972)
Knoebl, K., Victor Charlie, *The Face of War in Vietnam* (Pall Mall Press, 1967)

Lacouture, J., *Ho Chi Minh* (Penguin, 1968)
Lancaster, D., *The Emancipation of French Indo-China* (O.U.P., 1961)
Landau, D., *Kissinger: The Uses of Power* (Robson Books, 1974)
Lederer, W. J., *The Anguished American* (V. Gollancz, 1969)

McCarthy, M., *Vietnam* (Penguin, 1968)
  Hanoi (Penguin, 1969)
McCarthy, R. D., *The Ultimate Folly* (V. Gollancz, 1970)
Mailer, N., *The Armies of the Night* (Penguin, 1970)
Murray, R. (ed.), *Vietnam* (Eyre & Spottiswoode, 1965)
Murti, B. S. N., *Vietnam Divided* (Asia Publishing House, 1964)

O'Neill, R. J., *General Giap: Politician and Strategist* (Cassell, 1969)
Osborne, M., *Region of Revolt: Focus on Southeast Asia* (Penguin, 1971)

Reich, C., *The Greening of America* (Penguin, 1972)
Rosie, G., *The British in Vietnam* (Panther, 1970)
Roy, J., *The Battle of Dienbienphu* (Faber & Faber, 1965)

Salisbury, H., *Behind the Lines – Hanoi* (Secker & Warburg, 1967)

Schlesinger, A. M. Jr., *A Thousand Days* (André Deutsch, 1965)
   The Bitter Heritage, Vietnam and American Democracy 1941–1966 (André
   Deutsch, 1967)
Scigliano, R., *South Vietnam: Nation Under Stress* (Houghton Mifflin Co., 1963)
Segal, R., *America's Receding Future* (Penguin, 1970)
Sheehan, N. *et al.*, *The Pentagon Papers* (Bantam, 1971)
Sihanouk, N. & Burchett, W., *My War With The CIA* (Penguin, 1973)
Smith, R., *Viet-Nam and the West* (Heinemann Educational Books, 1968)
Snow, E., *The Other Side of the River* (V. Gollancz, 1963)

Thompson, R., *No Exit from Vietnam* (Chatto & Windus, 1969)

Warbey, W., *Ho Chi Minh* (Merlin Press, 1972)
Warner, D., *The Last Confucian* (Penguin, 1964)
Werth, A., *France 1940–1955* (Robert Hale, 1956)
Woddis, J., *Ho Chi Minh, Selected Articles and Speeches 1920–1967* (Lawrence &
   Wishart, 1969)

Zasloff, J. J. & Goodman, A. E., *Indochina in Conflict, A Political Assessment*
   (D. C. Heath, 1972)

INDEX

Abyssinia, 104
Accelerated Pacification Programme, 109
Acheson, Dean, 23
Adams, General, 109
AFL–CIO convention, 105
Agrovilles, 47, 55–6
Ancestor worship, 2, 3, 11, 56–7
Annam, 9, 10
Artillery bombardment, 83–4
Attlee, C. R., 17
Australia, 70

B-52 bombers, 83, 111, 113, 120
Ball, George, 110
Bao Dai, 15, 22, 36
Bertolino, Jean, 85
Bevin, Ernest, 19
Bidault, G., 26
Bienhoa, attack on, 76
Binh Xuyen, 19, 33
Bombing, of North Vietnam, 68, 69, 71, 73,
    77–8, 81, chapter 7 *passim*, 93, 117,
    118, 119, 120, 122
Bombing, of South Vietnam, 78, chapter 7
    passim
Borodin, Michael, 8, 9
Brest–Litovsk, treaty, 21
Brogan, Denis, 120
Buchwald, Art, 106
Buddhists, 59, 61, 89
Bundy, McGeorge, 64
Bundy, William, 71
Burma, 2, 3, 17, 25, 41, 70
Buttinger, J., 10, 44, 49

Cambodia, 70, 111, 112, 113, 131, 133
Cameron, James, 77–8
Can Lao Party, 38
Cao-Bang, Province, 15
Cao Dai, sect, 33
Ceasefire agreement (1973), 123ff.
Central Intelligence Agency, 63, 93, 110–
    11, 111–12
Chemical warfare, 84–5
Chiang Kai-shek, 10, 14
Chinese communists, 23, 24, 44
Chomsky, Noam, 103, 104
Chou En-lai, 128

Churchill, W. S., 17
Cité Hérodia, 18
Civilians, indiscriminate killing of, 85–6
Clemenceau, G., 8
Clifford, Clark, 80–1, 108
Cochinchina, 2, 3, 4, 11, 21
Cogny, General, 135
Cold War, 96
Collins, General Lawton, 33
Communist China, 41, 129, 130
Confucian system, 2, 3, 5
Congress, US, 71, 74, 75, 95, 98, 99, 100,
    111, 112, 115, 132, 133
Constellation, USS, 73
Constitutionalists, 11
Cultural Revolution, Chinese, 127–8
Czechoslovakia, Soviet invasion of, 127–8

D'Argenlieu, Admiral Thierry, 21
Declaration of Independence, Vietnamese,
    15, 16
Depression bomb, 133
Depuy, General, 80
De Soto patrols, 68, 73
Devillers, P., 16
Dienbienphu, 25, 26, 30, 135–6
Dominican Republic, 96
Dulles, John Foster, 25, 26, 33

Eden, Anthony, 26, 31
Eisenhower, Dwight D., 31, 33, 53, 97
Ellsberg, Daniel, 114

Fall, Bernard, 56, 83
Fitzgerald, Frances, 42, 56, 88, 90
Ford, Gerald, 133
Fort Bragg, 52
French colonialism, 2, 48
French conquest of Indochina, 2
Fulbright, Senator J., 74, 75, 96–8, 104

Gavin, General J., 100–1
Geneva Conference, 26, 27, 28, 30, 31, 32,
    35, 119, 123, 125, 136
Giap, General Vo Nguyen, 21, 25, 135–6
Goldwater, Barry, 71, 76
Gracey, General, 18, 19
Great Society, the, 95, 100, 105

Gruening, Senator, 74
Guam, 83

Halberstam, David, 48, 59–60, 79
Hammer, Ellen, 20
Ham Nghi, 5
Harkins, General Paul D., 58, 66, 68
Hartke, Senator, 100
Heren, Louis, 125
Herrick, Captain J., 74, 75
Hiroshima, 15
Hitler, Adolf, 13, 88
Hoa Hao, sect, 33
Ho Chi Minh (*see also* Nguyen Ai Quoc),
    8, 9, 13, 14, 15, 16, 20, 21, 22, 23, 24, 30,
    31, 41, 42, 44, 45, 46, 78, 94
Ho Chi Minh City, 134
Ho Chi Minh Trail, 77, 114
Honda, Katsuichi, 85–6
Hoopes, Townsend, 116
Hukbalahap Revolution, 27, 28, 32
Humphrey, Hubert, 106–7
Hungary, 104

Imperialist mentality, 1
India, 17, 19, 25, 70
Indochina, 2, 3, 10, 13, 16, 17, 19, 20, 21, 23,
    25, 26, 30, 104, 108, 116, 131, 136
Indochinese Communist Party, 9, 10, 11, 12

Japanese coup d'état (1945), 15
Johnson, Lyndon B., 1, 36, 55, 63, 65,
    chapter 6 *passim*, 82, 83, 94, 95, 96,
    100, 101, 102, 105, 106, 108, 113

Kennedy, Edward, 86–7
Kennedy, John F., 33, 50, chapter 5 *passim*,
    75, 84, 105
Kennedy, Robert, 107
Kent State University, 112
Khahn, General, 73, 87, 90
Khmer Rouge, 132
Khrushchev, Nikita, 51
Kissinger, Henry, 119, 125, 126, 128, 130,
    131
Korean War, 24, 26
Kuomintang Party, 6, 8, 10, 14, 20, 21
Ky, Nguyen Cao, 88, 90

Land reform, North Vietnam, 41–3, 49
Land reform, South Vietnam, 49
Landau, David, 126
Langguth, Jack, 85
Lansdale, Edward, 32, 33
Lao Dong Party, 30, 42, 46
Laos, 2, 25, 68, 70, 76, 77, 94, 108, 113,
    114, 131, 133, 135
Laski, Harold, 19
Lederer, W. J., 88
Le Duan, 46

Lenin, V. I., 9
Le Van Kim, 62
Lippmann, Walter, 32
Littauer, R., 118
Lloyd George, D., 8
Lodge, Henry Cabot, 62, 63, 64, 65, 66
Lon Nol, 111, 132
Ly Chanh Trung, 88

Maddox, USS, 73, 74
Malaya, insurgency in, 27, 28, 55
Malayan Communist Party, 27, 28
Mandarins, 3, 4, 5
Mao Tse-tung, 24
Marx, Karl, 11
Meiji emperors, 5–6
Military Advisory Command, 58
Military-Industrial complex, 97–8, 104
Minh, Duong Van, 133
Missionaries, 2, 3
Mohr, Charles, 85
Morale of US troops, 117
Morse, Senator Wayne, 74, 75, 77
Morton, Senator Thurston, 99
Mountbatten, Lord, 17
Muskie, Senator Edward, 118
Mussolini, Benito, 104
My Lai, 86, 109, 115–16
MacArthur, General Douglas, 19
McCarthy, Senator Joseph, 32, 103
McCarthy, Mary, 86
McConnell, General, 94
McGovern, Senator George, 118, 119
McNamara, Robert, 58, 63, 66, 70, 71,
    74, 75, 81, 93, 94, 98, 114

Nagasaki, 15
National Liberation Front, 48, 49, 50, 58,
    68, 85, 90–2, 95, 109, 110, 111, 123, 132
Nationalist movement, Vietnam, 11–12
Navarre, General, 135
Nazi-Soviet Pact, 13
Nehru, J., 19
New Zealand, 70
Nghe An, Province, 8, 9, 10, 12
Ngo Dinh Can, 38, 39
Ngo Dinh Diem, 33, 35, 36, 37, 38, 39,
    44, 45, 46, 47, 48, 49, 50, 53, 55, 56,
    58, 59, 61, 62, 63, 64, 65, 66, 83, 88,
    89
Ngo Dinh Luyen, 38
Ngo Dinh Nhu, 38, 39, 56, 61, 62, 63,
    65
Ngo Dinh Thuc, 38
Nguyen Ai Quoc, 8, 9, 10, 11, 12, 13
Nguyen Chahn Thi, 39
Nguyen Sinh Cung, 8
Nguyen Van Chau, 42
Nhu, Madame, 38, 39, 61, 62
Nicot, Colonel, 135

Nixon, Richard M., 75, 81, 106–7, chapter 9 *passim*, 123, 124, 125, 126, 130, 131, 133
Nolting, F., 61, 62
North Vietnam, 40, chapter 4 *passim*, 51, 76, 92, 94, 95, 113, 118–19, 120, 122, 133

Operation Barrell Roll, 77
Operation Castor, 135
Operation Plan 34A, 66–8, 73, 75
Operation Ranch Hand, 84
Operation Rolling Thunder, 77, 94, 114

Paris Peace Conference (1919), 8
Pathet Lao, 113, 132
Peaceful co-existence, 45, 46, 127
Pentagon Papers, 36, 69, 76, 80, 86, 114–15
People's Revolutionary Party, 91
Personalism, 38
Pétain, Marshal, 13
Pham Van Dong, 73
Phan Boi Chau, 5–8
Philippine Islands, 27, 70
Phoenix Programme, 110
Piroth, Colonel, 136
Pleiku, 77
Potsdam Conference, 16, 17, 18, 20
Provisional Revolutionary Government, 123, 124, 133

Race riots, 101, 105
Racial problem, USA, 101–2
Racist attitudes, in Vietnam, 116
Radford, Admiral, 25
Radical opposition to Vietnam War, 102–3
Refugees, 86–7
Reich, Charles, 96
Roosevelt, Franklin D., 16, 17
Rosie, George, 19
Rostow, W., 68
Rusk, Dean, 62, 63, 69, 74
Russo-Japanese War, 6

Saigon, in 1966, 90
Saigon Military Mission, 32
Schlesinger, Arthur, 103–4
Scholars' Revolt, 5
Seaborn, J. B., 73
Sheehan, Neil, 86, 115
Siam, 2
Sihanouk, Prince, 111–12, 113
Sino-Soviet split, 45, 71, 126–8
Sino-US détente, 128–31
Sirik Matak, 111
South Vietnam, chapter 3 *passim*, 44, 46, 48, 50, 51, 84, 110, 113, 116–17, 133

Soviet Union, 45, 104
Soviet-US détente, 127, 128
Special Forces, US, 51, 52
Spellman, Cardinal, 33
Stalin, J. V., 11, 13, 24
Stone, I. F., 69
Strategic Hamlets Programme, 55–7, 66
Suffren, 22
Sun Yat-sen, 6, 8

Taiwan, 70, 129–30
Taylor, Maxwell, 52–3, 58
Tet Offensive, 79, 80, 106
Thailand, 70, 83, 132
Thich Quang Duc, 59, 61
Thieu, Nguyen Van, 88, 90, 99, 108, 123, 124, 125, 132, 133
Ticonderoga, USS, 73
Tonkin, 10
Tonkin, Gulf of, 68, 71, 73, 75, 98, 99, 114
Tran Van Giau, 16
Truman, Harry S., 16, 17, 23, 32, 33
Truman Doctrine, 32
Truong Chinh, 42
C. Turner Joy, USS, 73

United States, 51, 53, 54, 62, 69–70, 71, 73, 81, 94, chapter 8 *passim*, 130
US casualties in Vietnam, 99, 108, 125, 133
US forces in Vietnam, 53, 78–81
US military expenditure in Vietnam, 100–1, 110, 125
US military leadership, 53, 54–5, 98–9

Vietcong, 48, 50, 51, 52, 55, 57–8, 59, 66, 68, 69, 70, 73, 76, 78, 80, 82, 83, 85, 109, 111
Vietminh, 13, 14, 15, 16, 18, 19, 20, 22, 24, 25, 26, 27, 28, 30, 31, 32, 33, 35, 37, 45, 47, 48, 49, 90, 135–6
Vietnam Revolutionary Alliance, 14
Vietnamese Communist Party, 9
Vietnamese Nationalist Party, 10
Vietnamization, 108, 109, 110, 125

Watergate, 75, 118, 126
Westmoreland, General, 78, 79, 80, 81
White Paper, State Department's, 1965, 68–9
Wilson, Woodrow, 8

Xo-viets, 9, 10

Yalta Conference, 16
Yen-Bay, 10

reflecting on the outcome of the previous 'settlement' at Geneva, they had in fact no illusions about achieving a peaceful solution. They were parading their political supremacy over Thieu, knowing that he intended to pursue the struggle not by votes but with bullets. On the eve of the ceasefire Kissinger had declared: 'It is clear that whether this agreement brings a lasting peace or not depends not only on its provisions, but also on the spirit in which it is implemented.'[9] While he was making that statement the US was doing its best to enable its client Thieu to continue the war. The old policy of Vietnamization, with the help of key US personnel masquerading as civilians, was going to keep the anti-communist flag flying in South Vietnam. As one correspondent predicted, ceasefire meant 'a South Vietnam divided into two hostile zones, where schemes for yet one more try at a military solution would surely be hatched'.[10]

Kissinger's negotiations, for which he received the Nobel Peace Prize, ensured that the war would continue without the overt presence of the United States. American troops, at least those in uniform, left South Vietnam and US prisoners-of-war were released. In those respects, the January agreements marked an important stage in the long history of the Vietnam War.

Louis Heren has described a discussion he had in 1969 with some of the key men in American government, for whom he had considerable admiration. 'I went on to recall,' he says, 'their civilized restraint, and avoidance of danger in Hungary, the Middle East and Czechoslovakia. What went wrong in Vietnam? There was a short silence, and a looking into now-empty glasses. Then with disarming candour, one of them said, "We thought we could win".'[11] For years the conviction that American power was irresistible had overridden all other considerations. In Vietnam, by the end of Nixon's first term in office it had cost the USA the lives of 46,000 men and some £50,000 million.[12] Even then, as already noted, Nixon, ignoring the terms of the ceasefire, continued US involvement by supplying experts and military equipment. However, the partial withdrawal was evidence of a recognition that the firepower of the US army and the advanced technology of their bomber fleets had failed to gain the victory so confidently expected when they were first extensively deployed in 1965. That fact had, as one observer commented, 'a sobering effect on the old American belief that everything is possible'.[13]

Confidence in the American system was shaken not only by events in Vietnam but also by another series of events in the United States itself. During 1973 the truth about the Watergate conspiracy began to emerge. It is now clear that there was a direct connection between that affair and the Vietnam War. The purpose of the political corruption was to guarantee the re-election of the President. Nixon and his fellow-conspirators appreciated that the war was the rock on which he might founder. They knew that if they ceased to pursue victory in Vietnam they would be almost certain of gaining an electoral victory in November 1972. However, they were determined to achieve a double triumph. The outcome of their overbearing self-confidence has been described in a recent biography of Kissinger, the main architect of Nixon's strategy. 'The Watergate revelations,' states Landau, 'proved quite clearly that with respect to Vietnam and other unpopular policies, many people in the White House wanted to have their cake and eat it too – that is, to pursue their policies without submitting to the risks which elected governments in democratic societies traditionally face . . . Nixon and Kissinger would not give the war up, and in so refusing they paved the way for Watergate. In retrospect, this Administration's Vietnam diplomacy . . . will be seen . . . as the genesis for the most horrible political scandal of our lifetime.'[14]

Some time must elapse before historians can assess adequately the ramifications of Watergate. Similarly, it is not possible at this juncture to gauge the full significance of the Vietnam War; this can only be an interim statement. Even now, however, some points seem clear. First, the war has shown the amazing tenacity of revolutionary nationalism in South Vietnam and the resilience of the society in North Vietnam. Secondly, it would appear that the prolongation of the conflict in Vietnam has caused a significant shift in world politics, particularly in the relationships of the three major powers which were most closely involved. This point may be illustrated by comparing the situation in 1965, when the Americans became deeply committed, with the international scene in 1973, when they carried out a major withdrawal from Indochina.

An outstanding feature in 1965 was the mutual hostility of the Soviet Union and China. The Sino–Soviet split, which had been widening for nearly a decade, was notable in the area of foreign policy. While the Soviet leaders persisted with their emphasis on